A MINISTERING MINISTRY

...BY...

W. R. WALKER

THE STANDARD PUBLISHING COMPANY

CINCINNATI, OHIO, U. S. A.

CONTENTS

AN INTRODUCTORY WORD

It is a perilous thing to preach and minister. In no other area of.human effort are such tremendous issues involved. There are but two possible destinies for an immortal soul, and these are separated by the infinite distances between heaven and hell. The very nature of the minister's assignment compels him to accept heavy responsibility for directing and leading men to God. That obligation was sworn to in his heart when he made final decision to preach and minister.

If he preach any other gospel than that which the Scriptures contain, or if he lead men astray by his example and counsels, he will answer to the charge of being a false representative of Christ—and the Day of Judgment will have no graver indictments than that. Ministering is, therefore, a sobering task.

The only bibliography suggested to the reader is the Bible—the only sourcebook consulted by the author in preparing these lectures. To him, the Bible is a book of authority in religion, and the only book entitled to be so classified. His one purpose has been to present the teaching of Christ and His apostles in their relation to the ministry of the gospel. Principles only have been dealt with, leaving details in homiletics, etc., out of the discussion in order to center thought on the great major objectives of all ministering.

These are trying days for the conscientious minister. In no previous age have there been so many compromising or clashing doctrines promulgated. Pulpit and platform, press and radio, are rivals in the arena where "some new thing" is proclaimed, each covetous of the applauding approval of a world seeking salvation by its own wisdom.

There is religious finality in the gospel of Jesus Christ, and all we know about that gospel is contained in the Bible.

This fact simplifies the work of the minister. He can clarify the thought and shape the living of men only by proclaiming the gospel of the Son of God with a conviction and passion born of an intelligent faith and a consecrated life. He has been commissioned by Christ to do just that. He has no alternative, either in message or program, to present.

This counsel to the minister who wants to see the kingdom of God established and strengthened: STICK TO YOUR OWN TASK.

CHAPTER I

Pre-Christian Backgrounds

Every human activity of one age roots in a background of earlier ages. Nothing is wholly new. Hence, what we are now doing, and why, may be understood and evaluated better when we are able to isolate and study the earlier, or earliest, source-factors of our own doings. This is certainly true of the work of ministering, whether investigated from the divine or human approach.

The sources of all reliable knowledge of pre-Christian ministries have been filed and catalogued in the Old Testament.

The study of non-Christian ministries, priestly or otherwise, does not come within the scope or purpose of this chapter. None of them should be treated as source materials for obtaining a correct understanding of Christian ministry.

In His providential preparation for the task of ministering, God did not lead either

7

prophet or priest up through the fogs of philosophic speculation, or out of the morasses of apostate practices, into positions of leadership in things pertaining to the life in the Spirit.

Non-Christian faiths have made no contribution to the Christian faith, in any respect. Nothing that is truly Christian can be traced to them—in doctrine, in ordinance, or in life. Eliminating them from our study, as fair scholarship compels us to do, we have nothing but Old Testament materials left for our study of "backgrounds." In these we can trace God's earliest plans for the salvation of man, through the employment of human help and mediation.

By comparison and contrast, examining both similitudes and dissimilitudes, some very illuminating facts are discovered.

Certain root ideas and foundational procedures concerning the work of ministering, as blue-printed in the Old Testament, foreshadow the function and method of ministering which Christ was to assign to His church, later.

Let us note some of them.

Two words in the Old Testament have been translated "to minister." Their etymology is significant, since etymology is to words what archæology is to history.

The first, *pelach,* has "to split" as its root meaning. (That is a rather dangerous idea for a minister to dwell upon, so we hasten on to its cognate meanings.)

It seems to describe the labor of a tiller of the soil, one who "splits" or "breaks" the hard earth in preparation for seed-planting. Hence, "to till, or serve" is a dictionary description of the term.

The other word translated "to minister" is *sharath,* almost identical in meaning with *pelach.*

These are both lowly words. The Old Testament "minister" was a subordinate, a laborer, often a slave. His specific duties might vary, according to the exigencies of the situation, but he was always taking orders, always obeying.

There are two words in the Old Testament which are translated "to preach." One, *basar,* means "to tell or bring good tidings." This is the word used in **Isa. 61: 1,** the passage read by Jesus in the Nazareth synagogue, where He declared: "Jehovah hath anointed me to preach good tidings to the meek." It seems to be a perfect equivalent for the Greek word to come into use later, and translated "to preach the gospel," or "evangelize."

The other term is *qara,* and is defined "to call, to proclaim, to preach." These two words appear to have been used interchangeably.

They emphasize a teaching, a warning, an oral service. It is an "enlightening" word.

Once, the noun "preacher" is used, in which the writer of Ecclesiastes so designates himself.

A verb from the same root was used by Jehovah, when He ordered the prophet to Nineveh "to cry" against that city.

The sermonic content of the word is evident.

No mistake can be made in affirming that the underlying significance of these Old Testament terms, is "to serve, in a subordinate position, in behalf of another." If, in obedience to an order given, the exercise of any authority was to be employed, it was manifestly limited to the commission under which the servant labored. The position of "minister" did not, in itself, carry any authority beyond that committed by the superior under whom the service was being rendered.

Levites, prophets, even kings, when used by Jehovah to carry out His programs and execute His will, always chose the humble words just studied to denote their relations to Him. They were "servants," regardless of the character of work entrusted to them.

We now proceed to a historical case study of the development of ministering through the pre-Christian centuries. God has always had His "ministers." With the single exception of that which was wrought by His Son, in the flesh, they have all been men. Angelic agencies might have been used, as they were occasionally in a supplementary measure, for instruction, admonition, exhortation, etc.; but for reasons of His own, God has delegated to chosen men, both the honor and responsibility of ministering, in His behalf, to their own kind.

Jehovah, Himself, delivered the first sermon to that new creature formed in His own image. It was in Eden, when He gave instruction concerning duties and warned against disobedience.

That sermon is a model in brevity and clarity.

Enoch was probably the pioneer preacher of our race. The apocryphal books bearing his name justify the deduction. His life was short, for that period, and those who knew him would mourn his early departure from earth, as we do the premature death of a promising young minister. He and God must have had important things to talk over on that day when they took a walk together and Enoch went on home with the Father.

He left a blessed heritage, however. Multitudes have been inspired to a closer walk with God by his example. (One is led to wonder whether there is significance in the statement: "Enoch walked with God, after he begat

Methuselah, three hundred years" [**Gen. 5: 22**].
Fatherhood exerts a tremendous influence on a
serious-minded preacher, a fact that certainly
has some bearing on the merits or perils of celi-
bacy.)

Noah next rises on the preacher-horizon.
In **2 Pet. 2: 5** he is called a "preacher of
righteousness." That is an illuminating statement. The Genesis record of his activities
tells of his preparation of the ark, commends
his personal piety, but omits mention of the
fact that he preached to his wicked neighbors
while building the vessel. Peter reveals his
work in "preaching" as being more than mere
denunciation and warning. He also urged
"righteousness" as a means of averting the
very catastrophe for which he was preparing.
True preaching will always be more than denunciation. It must show "a way out," else
all warning and exhortation would be puerile
or silly.

Noah's campaign of evangelism would be
discouraging to him, but he faithfully proclaimed his message, and thereby saved himself and seven of his family. More than one
preacher has saved himself by the recoil of his
sermon.

Moses was a great preacher and marvelous
minister, even though he did complain of being

"slow of speech" and "not eloquent." "Not eloquent" is, literally, "not a man of words." Does that imply that his deeds spoke more eloquently than his sermons? If so, he is a worthy example for the preacher of today.

"Slow of speech" means "heavy-worded." Does that suggest that he condensed his oration? If so, he has left another precedent for the student of homiletics.

He also was reluctant to enter the ministry when called. Others since his time have been hesitant, because the magnitude of the task unsteadied them. But when they were assured that God's flame was to enlighten, rather than to consume, they bared their feet to walk on the holy ground where souls were to be shepherded, leaving the shepherding of material things to others. Moses' example as minister has been a powerful recruiting influence in the enlistment of workers for Christ.

Samuel was "born to the ministry." He was a child of promise. Dedicated from birth, trained from early childhood, fitted both by temperament and ability for a life of ministering, he will ever be an inspiring study. It would be illuminating for us to know the extent to which connatal factors silently influence men to answer the ministerial call in this day. It is possible that the godly Hannahs send out more sons to preach the unsearchable riches of Jesus Christ than do the theological seminaries.

Samuel's ministry was a dual one. He served God, as prophet; and his nation, as kingly counselor. His early services as judge were rendered as God's chosen representative. Later, as political adviser to Saul, he always gave more consideration to the religious welfare of Israel than to mere political expediency.

He felt deep concern about his successors, and probably originated the "School of the Prophets," known in the Scripture as "sons of the prophets." Companies of earnest, spiritually-minded young men were chosen to live with or near the prophets that they might be their understudies. Their "masters" were men like Samuel, Elijah, Elisha. It is highly probable that definite courses of study and supervised training for their later prophetic duties were carried on.

One more concrete illustration of Old Testament ministering demands our notice. The prophet Nathan merits study and imitation. What a homily was that parable sermon to David, a homicidal king! His success in bringing the autocratic ruler to repentance would cheer his heart to his dying day.

Later, when David announced his plan to build the temple, Nathan used masterly tact in persuading the king to be content with assembling the materials and drawing the plans for the structure, and leaving the actual erection of it to his son, Solomon. The prophet was convinced that the son of Bathsheba was the logical successor to the throne, believing that the wisdom for which he was already famous, would enable him to conciliate the disaffected factions whose allegiance to David was never more than nominal. He reasoned that if such a national monument and center of worship as the temple promised to be were erected under Solomon, that enterprise would draw into one enthusiastic group the partisans of the lamented Saul, the ambitious Ephraimites, always seditious, and even the lesser princes of the royal house. If he did, history justified his foresight. His skill in dealing with the rebellious coup of Adonijah, revealed his possession of political strategy in an unusual degree.

Thus, in one man, we see combined the dual phases of ministering demanded in a state where church and state were united.

His courage and unselfish devotion to his prophetic ministry have been an inspiration to loyal ministers of the Word through three millenniums.

It will be profitable to examine with some care two or three notable cases of Old Testament ministries, that additional background material may be studied.

The ministry of Joseph, both to Jehovah and in behalf of his brethren, merits special attention. He was the first minister with a burning passion for "unity," so far as our records go. God's providential preparation for that type of a ministry began with an endorsement of Jacob's choice of Joseph as heir to the patriarchal blessing and family head. Jacob announced his choice to the other sons by clothing Joseph with "a garment with long sleeves"— princely uniform. Jehovah approved by revealing His will to Joseph in dreams. From the very first approach he made to his brethren, to the last day of his life, he seems to have been moved by a sense of responsibility for uniting his family into a nation, instead of permitting it to scatter into wandering nomadic families or tribes. Every move he made, in both his personal dealings with his brethren and as viceroy of Egypt, can be understood if this central purpose be kept in mind. He reveals his dreams to both his father and brothers, with not a trace of presumption, no feeling of superiority, no arrogance or demand. He seems subdued, almost overcome, by the hint found in the visions. It is easy to see why the older brothers were envious and plotted his removal. The father was puzzled, but not displeased, when he himself was assigned the role of an inferior, acknowledging the authority of his son, contrary to all tribal and patriarchal precedent.

Joseph's treatment of his brethren when they appeared in Egypt for food was masterly strategy. "What sort of men are they now?" His last encounter with them disclosed their jealousy of each other, envious, quarreling, murderous. Have they changed in character? They are now in a position where they are compelled to bow before him as a civil authority. Are they also ready to accept a ministry, in spiritual and national life, the central purpose of which is to weld them into a nation united under Jehovah? If assured that God had been making providential preparation for them by raising him to the exalted station he then held, would they co-operate in his program for uniting them? Will they follow Jehovah's plan?

To ascertain the sort of men they are, he roughly orders Benjamin imprisoned, to be kept as his slave. Will they care? Though the youngest son, Benjamin had probably been chosen as Joseph's successor by Jacob because he was the child of his beloved Rachel. If the others have not changed, they will be glad to leave him there, and resume their contest

among themselves for supremacy. Imagine
Joseph's emotions when Judah, the one who
had been responsible for his being sold as a
slave, bows before him to make that plea for
Benjamin's release, offering to be a hostage
for him, and if necessary, to bring his entire
family into slavery, if only Benjamin be given
freedom. That plea, one of the most eloquent
and masterly in history, gave Joseph the answer
he was waiting to hear. These men are now
disciplined, ready to serve with him, as he
serves Jehovah only.

It is now clear to both him and them, how
God's providence had brought him into Egypt
to "serve" or "minister" to them in an hour of
terrible need. They accept his leadership without protest or envy. Their families are brought
down for still further welding into a brotherhood in the fires of slavery and common suffering. Like any true minister of today, Joseph
served, in his leadership capacity, because he
was convinced he had been called of God for
that service, and he loved his brethren, notwithstanding their sins.

The ministries of Moses and Joshua are
best interpreted as being a continuation of
Joseph's divinely authorized program for the
uniting of Jacob's descendants into a nation.
They saw God's purpose for this people, and

dedicated themselves to its realization. Their ministry was in the name of Jehovah, and rendered in behalf of His people. That ideal has been a constant factor in all approved ministering till this very hour.

A word should be said concerning David, who was a "minister of song" as well as prophet and king. The finest thing about David's ministry is disclosed in the expression that he was "a man after God's own heart." He loved truth, righteousness, justice, and was willing to do what God desired of him. He was a seeker after God's will. God could forgive even a heinous sin of the flesh, because David knew how to repent religiously.

God loves the minister who seeks "God's own heart," rather than his own exaltation; who seeks God's own programs and plans instead of those prescribed by ecclesiastics.

The order of "ministers" we usually call "prophets" served in important capacities in Old Testament times. They were both seers and preachers of righteousness. They were advisers to rulers in religious, social and political life, and appear to have been the usual mediums through whom Jehovah revealed Himself on special occasions, or for special reasons.

The sermonic deliverances of Isaiah and Micah come from hearts filled with evangelistic passion. They are clarion calls to repentance, and show a conviction that Jehovah will ultimately be universally acknowledged as the only God. They tried to lift their people out of the narrowness of racial intolerance.

Amos preached the omnipresence, omnipotence and righteousness of Jehovah, insisting that He is absolute in power and control. Yet His power was being limited in the lives of men, because their social injustice, greed and luxurious living had crowded out true religion, despite their sacrifices and offerings and their strict attention to ritual.

Hosea, probably prompted by a special revelation, presented Jehovah's complaint against Israel in telling allegory. His statement that Jehovah commanded him to "take a wife of whoredom and children of whoredom" is surely not biographical. It is unthinkable that Jehovah should humiliate a loyal prophet minister by such an order. Israel's unfaithfulness to Him who had espoused the nation to Himself was portrayed in that figure which would stir to repentance if any power of persuasion could.

His prophecy is an ideal example of the place and effectiveness of allegory.

Brief notice must be taken of a rather unusual and somewhat perplexing statement concerning Old Testament ministries in **Isa. 44:28**

—**45: 1,** in which Cyrus is called "my shepherd" by Jehovah. The employment of one who was not a worshiper of Jehovah, or at least not an exclusive worshiper of Him, as a "shepherd" to care for His people is unexpected. But the statement is there. It suggests that God sometimes uses certain instrumentalities or personalities as "ministers," in which such service to Him is only incidental. It is doubtful whether Cyrus cared for Israel because they were Jehovah's peculiar people, and "shepherded" them to please the God of Israel. But his political situation was such that he could befriend them by a royal decree enabling them to restore the house of God, thus using his political power to aid a people who had found favor with him while in captivity. The incident is an interesting illustration of how God sometimes uses men to achieve His purposes, even when they may have had motives other than a desire to please Him as their chief incentive.

The activities of Old Testament prophets may be summed up as having been motivated by one supreme objective—to engender and maintain in both personal and national life *a sense of responsibility to God alone in religion,* and *righteousness* in *all* their *human relationships.* Without exception, these minister-

ing servants insisted that Jehovah was a
jealous God, tolerating no rivals. He alone
was God, not of Israel only, but of all mankind.
No more slanderous misrepresentation of Israel's conception of God has been made than
that, to them, He was a tribal, local, or national
god. Not one single Old Testament passage,
fairly exegeted, compels such an interpretation. He was theirs, not in an exclusive sense,
but because they were willing to follow Him.
In every reference made to Him in Scripture,
Jehovah is conceded universality. It was He
that "made the heavens and the earth"—certainly not a local or tribal achievement! To
Him "all the ends of the earth" were held
responsible, and would ultimately turn to Him.
All other deities were contemptuously called
"no gods." It is not an unfair generalization
to affirm that the chief task of the Old Testament prophets was to proclaim and defend
monotheism, with all its implications. They
traced every national disaster to apostasy, assuredly a more basic explanation than one that
is purely political. The Jehovah of the prophets
may be indifferent as to who rules, or what
form of government he represents, but He
demands that first place be given to Him in
everything. Isaiah quotes Jehovah: "There is
no God beside me."

We next notice a phase of ministering, essential to worship under the law as written in the Old Testament, entrusted to the priesthood. Originally, priestly duties or privileges seem to have been general, or vested in the heads of families. The priest was one duly authorized to minister at the altar, or about sacred things. He presided at the offering of sacrifices. Confession of sins, which necessitated an offering, was made by him, or by the worshiper in his presence. He was a mediator between the sinner and God. The Bible does not so state, but God doubtless instituted the altar as the first vehicle of worship for primitive man and instructed in the proper use of it.

Had no such teaching been given, the acceptance of Abel's offering and the rejection of Cain's, can not be explained.

In these instances, each seems to have officiated at his own altar service. It is idle to speculate on its probable religious significance to them, but they were obeying a command, and that gave opportunity to test the quality of their obedience.

Later, either by divine command, or by general agreement as to the fitness of the plan, the father of the family appears as one with priestly obligations to his own. Patriarchs like Abraham and Jacob, so officiated. Perhaps theirs was not an exclusive right, but delegated to them with the thought that the investment of the family or tribal head with religious responsibility would be a restraining influence in the exercise of his social and economic control. It was a sobering trust.

Whoever offered a sacrifice, by that act assumed a priestly status. With nothing to offer, he was no priest. The Roman Catholic priest is logical in insisting on calling the Mass a sacrifice. By that claim his authority over the parish is maintained, for without him they can not worship.

It is a similar desire on the part of some Protestant ecclesiastics which leads them to look upon the minister as having priestly standing, with exclusive rights to administer the ordinances. Some even conduct a sort of sterilized "confessional," vainly yearning for priestly confidences.

Some preside at infant dedication services as a sort of quieting gesture for the benefit of those accustomed to Romish procedure, encouraging the priestly conception of the ministry thereby. Such compromising imitation of an un-Scriptural ritual and implied acquiescence in a theological error is regrettable. Substitutes seldom satisfy, anyhow. Proxy religious acts are of doubtful spiritual value.

When the time was ripe for the merging of twelve tribes into a national family, God chose Aaron to be high priest for all Israel, his sons to be helpers and successors, and the tribe of Levi as underpriests. The selection of one man to be high priest, was the best means of developing and perpetuating the national ideal. It would unify them in worship, and where that condition obtains, defection and rebellion are least likely.

Aaron's close association with Moses, the civil ruler as well as revelator, assured a practical union in religious and political life. Throughout the entire period of Israel's national existence, chief priests and civil rulers were associated in governmental affairs.

Heb. 5: 1-4 emphasizes the fact that priests were divinely chosen and appointed. It was God Himself, not a hierarchy, who made the choice. There is a principle involved in this declaration, well worthy of the study of ecclesiastically-minded folk today. It hints that the selection of a family and tribe was designed, in part at least, to prevent the rise of an ecclesiastical organization. *That which is hereditary can not be ecclesiastically created.*

Rules of procedure, and precedence in rank, etc., would be necessary, of course, but they would depend upon the birth status and would not be subject to manipulation by ambitious men.

While mediatorial work was the primary function of priests, they were also the teachers and educators of the people. Their support being provided by the tithes, they were free to devote themselves to the social and intellectual life of their nation, as well as to its religious needs. It is safe to assume that they were not mere parasites living off the earnings of the working tribes. The equally arduous and more exhausting labor in intellectual and religious areas, if faithfully performed, would insure against moral flabbiness and materialistic luxury.

Turning to the New Testament, it is impossible to find close parallel between the priestly function of the Old Testament regime and the ministerial duties to be performed by the "servants" of the church.

The church has its high priest in Christ Himself. That office He still holds, hence, He has no successors. By His entrance into the Holy of Holies, heaven itself, with His own blood as our sin-offering, He has opened the way for all His followers to officiate for themselves in the church, as is so clearly set forth in the priestly argument found in the Hebrew letter (**Heb. 4: 14—10: 39**).

In the tenth chapter, the writer urges "bold entrance" into the "holy place," where none but priests were privileged to go and offer up their own sacrifices. This assured all those whom he addressed (Christians in general) that Christ had opened up the way into the holy place, into which they might enter with their own sacrifices, officiating for themselves.

This teaching is in agreement with other New Testament passages. Peter, in **1 Pet. 2: 5, 9,** calls his readers "a holy priesthood," "a royal priesthood." Higher mediatorial rights than here implied can not be conceived of for man, and they are universal to Christians.

Rev. 1: 6, also takes for granted the universal priesthood of believers.

In **Rom. 12: 1, 2,** Paul exhorts all Christians to present their "bodies a living sacrifice," thus exercising priestly functions.

The only "sacrifice" a Christian can offer is his "body"—the physical medium through which he does all his work in this life—and he is the only one who can do that.

Thus, the three greatest apostles agree in their assignment of priestly responsibilities and privileges to all Christians.

They seem to think of Christians as priests of equal rank; subordinate to Christ, the High Priest, but not to any human priest.

Furthermore, these priestly rights, like those under the law of Moses, are hereditary, all "brethren" of the high priest being entitled to them, by virtue of their birthrights. We are "joint-heirs with Christ," "if children, then heirs," etc., because we are Christ's. If all Christians are hereditary priests, as the New Testament unmistakably teaches, and of equal rank, then no place can be found for "the minister as priest," in any special or official sense. Under Christ, as under the law, that which is hereditary can not be ecclesiastically created. This fact negates the validity of all claims to peculiar or official priestly rights by the "clergy." It follows, therefore, that churches which regard the teaching and practice of the apostles as authoritative, must insist that every Christian has a divine right to officiate in every act of worship, or in the administration of any ordinance. They will also oppose every movement to elevate one above another in ecclesiastical power or control.

No survey of pre-Christian backgrounds which throw light on the work of ministering would be complete without attention being given to the synagogue.

This institution, at the time of Christ, had become an established organization, almost as widespread as the "dispersion" itself, yet entirely without Old Testament sanction. Its origin is uncertain, but probably it came into being during the captivity. Wherever Jews went, the synagogue went. Every city of size or commercial importance had one or more. They were numerous in Palestine, even Jerusalem being estimated by some to have had four hundred—probably an exaggeration. The membership in a synagogue was often made up of a "selected" group; e. g., we read of "The Synagogue of Freedmen," a congregation whose personnel was probably composed of former slaves. The "Cyrenians," the "Alexandrians," the "Cilicians," et al., had an organization for natives or citizens of those cities, respectively. Certain social or national or cultural groups seem to have preferred those in their own strata as members. Such a condition was doubtless both wise and fruitful, and assuredly made for congeniality.

The synagogue provided for the religious and, to some extent, the cultural needs of the congregation composing its membership. Here the devout gathered for instruction in the law, for mutual edification and encouragement, for such worship as did not require priestly offerings, to plan for the relief of the needy, and to administer such disciplinary measures as were deemed necessary for the common good.

It was natural that in such an assembly, preaching should be introduced. It would grow out of teaching and exhortation.

The most stressed phase of synagogue worship was that of teaching the law. The ritual provided for prayers also. Consideration of matters affecting the lives of the members occupied some time.

The rise and spread of these assemblies throughout the empire may be regarded as providential, even though without direct divine order. They provided a beginning place for the founding of churches in numerous instances. In them, Jesus and His disciples taught whenever opportunity afforded. Some churches were probably born in them.

It was but natural that when those members who accepted Jesus as Christ were "cast out of the synagogue," they should organize themselves into working and worshiping groups similar to those from which their religious relations were severed.

In form of organization, therefore, the synagogue created a pattern for the first churches. It was not the tabernacle, not the temple, which provided ritual or precedent for the church, but the synagogue. It is significant that no place was given to a "priest" in the synagogue gathering or organization.

The officiary of the synagogue consisted of six classes:

First, men of maturity and experience, held in esteem by the congregation, were chosen to manage the congregational activities. They were called "elders." In addition to the exercise of general supervision over the body, they probably were granted disciplinary authority. Excommunication was decreed by them, and ratified by the synagogue. On their shoulders rested the heaviest official responsibilities.

Each synagogue had one or more "rulers," probably chosen from the "elders." The ruler presided at the public services, selected the reader of the Scriptures for the day, and named the "preacher." He was the moderator of the assembly. When Jesus "stood up to read" in the synagogue at Nazareth (**Luke 4:16**), He did it upon the invitation of the "ruler."

The one who led in prayer was called "the delegate of the congregation." No better descriptive term for that delicate trust and honor has been coined. If those who lead worshiping groups in prayer today could be made to feel that they are actually delegates of the assembly, appearing in its behalf before God, an uplifting spiritual service would be assured. A conscience on this would come near solving our worship problems. Emphasis on form, ritual, arrangement of sanctuary furniture, etc., will never solve them. At least, they never have done so. "Almoners" gathered and distributed gifts for poor relief.

In synagogue worship, passages declaring the unity of God were read or recited, such as are found in **Deut. 6: 4-9; 11: 13-21.**

This was followed by a cycle of prayers, after which prescribed passages from the law and the prophets were read.

The sermon, followed by the benediction, to which all the congregation responded with an "Amen," closed the worship.

This brief outline of synagogue procedure will enable us to see how largely the worship and other activities of the early churches were patterned after the accepted practices of the Jewish assemblies.

CHAPTER II

Jesus' Teaching on Ministering

The preceding chapter dealt with certain pre-Christian phases of ministering, as found in the Old Testament Scriptures and Jewish institutions. Authoritative teaching and example on the subject, however, are found in the New Testament, to which attention is now given.

Naturally and logically, such an investigation must begin with a survey of the teaching and work and method of Jesus Himself. That a measurable similarity between the ministry of Jesus and that of His chosen disciples exists, is indicated in His Gethsemane prayer— "As thou didst send me into the world, even so sent I them into the world" (**John 17: 18**). He was both their authority and their model.

There was definite order in the program of Jesus in His ministering. Luke so asserts in **Acts 1: 1,** "The former treatise I made, O Theophilus, concerning all that Jesus began

both to do and to teach, until the day in which
he was received up." There is significance in
that order: *"do,* and *teach."* One who has
wrought a successful work himself is better
qualified to instruct another how to proceed
than is one who only knows the task theore-
tically. In the "fulfilling of all righteousness"
Jesus left us a God-approved example for both
the method and the content of ministering. But
the example preceded the instruction. In
every successful ministry, serving precedes
teaching. The ministerial life must always be
more eloquent than the tongue.

Notwithstanding points in common, however, Jesus' ministry differed in certain vital
respects from that of His apostles, and even
more from that which has been committed
to us.

"He taught as one having authority" was
the comment of those who heard His Sermon
on the Mount (**Matt. 7: 29**). That authority
was inherent in Him, and such authority abides
in Deity only. The inference is obvious. His
teaching had the approval of God. Men began
to raise questions concerning His unique personality early in His ministry. They saw wind
and wave, disease and death, demon and
saint, angel and God acknowledge and respect
His authority. His spectators and His audi-

ences were astounded at what they saw and heard. As the Son of God, He did and taught the will of God with first-hand knowledge.

No such authority was ever vested in apostle, prophet, evangelist, pastor or church. Certain phases of authority He delegated to all the above named groups of ministering agencies; but they are not like His in either origin or assignment. All authority rightfully exercised by them, is limited to that delegated by Him, to be used in trust.

Jesus' ministry was creative in a unique sense. He came to introduce a new life into the world. This life He demonstrated in Himself, revealed the process of its impartation to men, and committed to His apostles the responsibility of proclaiming that plan to the world. They were so successful in their work that Paul, looking upon some of his beloved converts, said of them, "If any man is in Christ, he is a new creation: the old things are passed away; behold, they are become new" (**2 Cor. 5:17**). Jesus Himself could impart this new life; the apostles, and we today, can only instruct concerning His power and plan for its impartation. We dare not originate anything in religion, being responsible for the proclamation of Christ's message precisely as He has had it recorded for us.

Jesus' ministry differed from ours in another respect. He performed miracles, demonstrating His divinity and authenticating His teachings thereby. His apostles and certain of their associates were granted similar power, to be used with discretion. The ministry of today is not so endowed.

We have no need for it. Those who reject the gospel in this age, after nineteen hundred years during which its power in the hearts of men has been successfully proven, would "not believe though one should rise from the dead" and confirm it. That is literally true. If a dead man should return with a story, why should we believe him? There is no evidence that death changes character, and if a liar should come back, we should be justified in discounting all he might say. Death did not change either the character or personality of Jesus. There is not a hint in the Word of God that it will change any other.

Jesus' own resurrection proved Him to be the Son of God, because He prophesied He would rise in demonstration of His power over death—a very different thing from being the subject on which such power might be exercised by another.

The testimony on which our faith rests, is sufficient and convincing.

It is germane to our purpose to study Jesus' miracles more fully, to ascertain what relationship they held to His gospel message. Otherwise stated, was His mission to minister to men's bodies, or to their souls? Was He primarily concerned about social service or spiritual redemption?

The testimony of the New Testament itself is that His healing ministry (including all His "wonders and signs") was always secondary, and for apologetic purposes. It retired into the background just as soon as it had summoned an audience and introduced the divine Personality. Miracle, even when the element of compassion entered into it, was but a portal servant to open the heart's door, welcome the guest, wash the dust of ignorance and skepticism from his feet and prepare him for an audience with his rightful King, in some inner chamber of His love. **Mark 2:1-12** may be cited as an illustration. Good reason exists for believing that the paralytic in Capernaum was brought to Jesus suffering more from a sense of sin-guiltiness than from his palsy. Jesus' first word to him, "Son, thy sins be forgiven thee," justifies the belief. It is conceivable that he might have been carried back to his home with soul relief, but without physical healing, had it not been for the reasoning of the scribes who branded His word of absolution as blasphemy. The paralytic provided the opportunity to prove Jesus' authority to forgive sins—confessedly a divine prerogative. "That ye may know that the Son of man hath authority to forgive sins," He said to His critics; turning to the palsied man He commanded, "Arise, take up thy bed and walk." Clearly, the physical miracle was wrought to substantiate His claim to authority in the intangible and unseen realm of soul-guilt. It does not appear that He ever healed a single individual from sheer compassion. There were multitudes of afflicted folk in Palestine whom He did not heal. It is safe to affirm that not one single surplus miracle was performed by Him. Each one fitted perfectly into the situation in which it is found. Lift it out of its setting, and it would appear to be something "dragged in." One is compelled to think a divine providence arranged for each "wonder and sign" in advance of its manifestation. Let us illustrate this with a reference to the instance where Peter found the coin in the fish's mouth (**Matt. 17: 24-27**). Here is a "fisherman's miracle." Nothing could have been more convincing to a man of that trade. The Man who gave Peter that order must have known where that piece of money was, just where and when to direct the casting of the hook to catch it. This would prove to a fisherman that nothing can happen on earth that is not pigeon-holed in heaven, and that Jesus has access to the files! (The believing minister of today can inform his audience that Jesus knows as much about the location of money now as He did then. But if the preacher thinks Peter caught a fish worth a shekel and sold it, trying to allegorize the miracle out of history, he should delete this record from his New Testament and deliver ethical essays instead of trying to preach.)

A further word about Jesus' miracles may be relevant. His warning, "See that thou tell no man," was often given. This prohibition was given in all sincerity. Discussion of the miracles would lead to speculation concerning the probable explanation, affording His enemies an opportunity to suggest that they were works of magic or sleight-of-hand performances. Jesus desired the miracle itself to stand out before all, but forbade detailed discussion of it until the proper time came to bring its testimony to bear on His divine claims.

An interesting personal experience of some years ago, is to the point here by way of illustration. The foreman in a stone quarry in the neighborhood had planned to dislodge from

its rock bed a rectangular block weighing
hundreds of tons. He wanted to break all
records in that type of quarrying. He had
drilled some half a hundred perpendicular holes
from the top of the ledge he was working,
to a depth of eighteen or twenty feet. Each
drill hole was then creased in a line parallel
to the face of the ledge. The same number
of holes were driven in horizontally from the
face, joining the perpendicular ones at the
bottom, all creased similarly in line. Exactly
the right amount of blasting powder was
tamped into every hole, fuses placed, and wired
to a central battery. Too much powder would
shatter the rock; too small a charge would fail
to lift the block from the ledge. Painstaking
work by skilled hands alone could guarantee
the success of the undertaking. When all was
in readiness, the author, a personal friend of
the foreman, was invited to press the button
which would release electric energy to every
drill hole at the same time. The experiment
was a perfect success. Electric sparks leaped
simultaneously to every prepared charge of
powder, and the immense block of rock was
thrust forward far enough that quarrymen
could work on five faces of it.

Jesus went about over Palestine, leaving in
every community some miracles as proof of

His divine Sonship. Each one was an unignited powder charge left there to await the electric news of His resurrection. When His disciples returned later with that gospel message, the block of unbelief would be lifted from every honest heart. Every miracle was authenticated and its evidential power increased a thousand fold by the resurrection. The proclamation of Jesus' healings, however, was no part of the message He entrusted to His disciples.

Let us now note the subject matter of Jesus' personal teaching. When we contemplate the infinite range of His knowledge, the limited area of His teaching is astonishing. As joint Creator of the world, He knew all the secrets of nature, the laws by which it works, how to regulate and control it, both in order and disorder. Yet in all His teachings, He made no reference to scientific truth, except to illustrate some phase of His kingdom. His ministry was devoted to just one theme: the contrasting facts of *sin* and *righteousness*. He never invaded any other realm of human interest. Religious and moral obligations monopolized His thought in speaking. He seems to have been concerned about one thing only so far as our race is concerned: to locate and apply the knife to sin. What a soul-

surgeon He was! What an experience it would
be to watch Him enter a consultation room
of modern quacks of "culture," listen to their
proposed social, educational behavioristic,
humanistic, or "what have you" prescriptions
for the relief of the patient writhing in the
paroxysms of sin! When all had finished He
would calmly say, "Gentlemen, this sin comes
not out but by prayer and the power of God
abiding in me." He knew that sin, whether
religious or moral, must be treated with divine
remedies. Not one can be cured by human
wisdom or material controls.

Jesus' sermons were always directed to the
inner life. He refused to deal with special
or peculiar situations when consulted about
them. Approached by one of the heirs of an
estate and importuned to "speak with the
brother that he divide the inheritance," He
flatly refused to be an arbitrator. "Man, who
made me a ruler or a judge over you?"—is
somewhat curt and rebuking. Following His
own question, before the stunned inquirer could
recover from the blow, He proceeded to give
the dissatisfied complainer a lecture on the
perils of covetousness (**Luke 12: 13, seq.**). He
was more interested in one's attitude toward
property than He was in its distribution.
Preachers may find a lesson here.

If at times He gave what might be deemed specific teaching, He was actually employing the common figure of metonymy, in which the particular was used for the general. As, for illustration, when He taught, "If any man would go to law with thee, and take away thy coat, let him have thy cloak also," He was assuming that the court judgment would assess the amount due the plaintiff from the defendant. Jesus made that concrete incident the basis for teaching that, in payment of a debt, or in making restitution, one should do more than strict justice demands.

He never gave out information merely to gratify curiosity on the part of an audience. When asked, "Lord, are they few that are saved?" He replied with a rebuke which the questioner would not forget: "Strive to enter in by the narrow door." It is a fine example of courteous, but unmistakable, reproof of curious meddling into the affairs of others.

Perhaps, in a sense, His conversation with Nicodemus is a parallel instance. Nicodemus began with a gentlemanly challenge to Jesus to confidentially reveal to him the *source* of His power by saying, "Rabbi, we know that thou art a teacher come from God." This was an Oriental indirection inviting Jesus to commit Himself as to His real personality. Instead

of granting the request, Jesus X-rayed the soul
of the proud Sanhedrist, and prescribed: "Nicodemus, you must be born from above."   Not
even with a doctor of the law would Jesus
waste time in discussing the source of His
power until the doctor's heart was in proper
condition. He refused a philosophical exchange
of ideas or theories and directed the interview
to a consideration of the one thing that had
brought Him to earth—making men over into
new men. One can imagine the humiliation of
the night visitor at this unexpected turn, but
we admire him for remaining to hear Jesus
through. We dare indulge the belief that he
profited also by his opportunity.

In all His ministry, Jesus appears to have
had but one objective—the religious one of
bringing souls into right relations with God.
That accomplished, all their human relationships would of necessity be right. The soul
living in fellowship with God, through Him
as God's Son, had "life"; the soul shut away
from God by sin was "dead." To be in Christ
was to possess the "abundant life" which He
came to give, and which had but little to do
with physical comforts, intellectual apprecia-
tions, an understanding of æsthetic values or
the enjoyment of political privileges. If these
things were indispensable to abundant living,

Jesus Himself lived a spiritually starved existence. He had none of the "things" about which we hear much as contributory factors to real "life." Not that such things are antagonistic to His program, nor incompatible with it; but simply that they are not an essential part of it. Jesus measured "life" by the divine standard of "goodness." Attainments, achievements, experiences, joys, etc., in other areas of human interest neither added to nor took from "life," as He lived it. Like His saying about a rich man and a needle's eye, this may be a "hard saying" for some, but it is true. By keeping this fact in mind, the minister may be able to bring comfort to distressed souls who, without such an outlook on life, would be tempted to despair or rebellion. He can honestly remind them that the abiding rewards for service are bestowed in the life hereafter, not in the present. They may be encouraged to "endure by looking unto the recompense of reward."

A frail scrub woman who cleans offices at night that she may eat bread honestly earned, giving motherly care to her own as best she can, may have neither time nor native endowment enabling her to share a poet's rapture over a tree, or cloud or stream. But by living the consecrated life, she may have an "abundance" of what Jesus came to give—reconciliation and fellowship with God through the forgiveness of sin, and that is "life."

The minister who confines his labors to the task of showing the "dead" the way to "life" will be kept very, very busy, and will experience a joy in his ministry that is deep, rich, blessed.

He will be "sharing the joy of his Lord," according to promise.

No fact of the New Testament teaching stands out more clearly than that, in Jesus' agenda, what we call "social service" was secondary and subsequent to discipleship.

One is tempted to wonder whether the record of the feeding of the five thousand, so carefully preserved by all the Evangelists, was not left as an object lesson. Having eaten to satiety from the miraculously multiplied loaves and fishes on one day, the same crowd followed Him to another location on the lake the next day, expecting a repetition of His miracle. Instead of feeding them, He began to preach from the text, "Work not for the food which perisheth, but for the food which abideth unto eternal life, which the Son of man shall give unto you." As He spoke, the audience gradually drifted away, some to their nets, some to their fields, some to their merchandise, until at last

His near disciples only remained. What pathos in His voice when He asked, "Will ye also go away?"! He had fed thousands one day to have a text for a sermon on "The Bread of Life" to be preached the following day. His miracle had served to assemble the audience again, but it did not convert a single soul, so far as the record indicates. When no more loaves and fish were on hand for distribution, the people lost interest in the Man who wanted them to *be good*. It is not improbable that this lengthy narrative has been left to us as an object lesson on the futility of attempting to win men to Christ by feeding and housing programs. Expensive blunders might have been avoided, and discouraging experiences prevented, had the church always depended more upon the preaching of the gospel, as Christ authorized, than upon schemes of social reform and amelioration.

Having studied Jesus' program and message content for Himself, as basic to a correct understanding of the ministry He desires us to render, let us now look into His instructions on this point. Just what did He have in mind when talking about "ministering"?

The word He used most frequently in referring to it is that revealing one, *diakonia.* In the broad sense it denotes any service to another, especially that which is menial. In His choice of this humble term, Jesus dignified all honest labor. He removed the curse of servility from it by lifting it into the region of spiritual greatness.

His ministers were to "serve." They were counseled to take seats near the foot of the table. A death sentence on ambition was pronounced in that advice. Should an invitation to a more honorable seat be extended, it might be graciously accepted, but He did not suggest that the guest be overly anxious to catch the eye of a curtsying waiter who might say, "Friend, come up higher"!

With a stinging rebuke, apparently in the presence of the other disciples, He refused the request of Salome and her ambitious sons for preeminent positions in His kingdom (**Matt. 20: 20-28**). They were informed that positions of trust and responsibility in His eternal kingdom would be *won,* not parceled out to favorites, as compliments. They would be conferred upon those who had served best in humble positions. He made it clear that God's proletarians might outrank man's aristocrats. "Whosoever would become great among you, shall be your minister; and whosoever would be first among you shall be your servant; even as the Son of man came not to be ministered unto, but to minister, and to give his life a ransom for many." Jesus approved the desire to be truly great; but He was deeply concerned that greatness be sought in those activities wherein Godlike greatness might be developed. He Himself was not too proud to use the basin and towel, even at the end of His personal ministry. To Jesus belongs the distinction of having discovered and worked the richest mine of greatness—unselfish service. It is the most profitable vein of spiritual gold open to any minister. He may stake out his own claim and work it to any extent he may wish, and each day's labor will insure a rich yield.

The Scripture passage cited above forbids one to enter the ministry through the door on the lintel of which is carved the word "CAREER." This ideal will lead him to strive for the big, the spectacular, the unusual, the successful, the remunerative. It will cause him to be more anxious to succeed than to do the Father's will. He will be found seeking the prominent pulpit or ecclesiastical preferment. He will want to "be somebody." The first question asked in every situation is likely to be, "What is best for *me?*" He may be willing to serve, provided it be in directing great enterprises, or where he is granted controlling or

directing authority in some "kingdom enterprise." (What ecclesiastical crimes have been
committed in the name of "kingdom promotion"!)

He looks upon the ministry as a "profes-
sion." That word is too dignified, hence cheap-
ening, for a true servant.

Not infrequently the youth gifted as an
orator possessing an attractive personality, of
good character, etc., is urged to enter the ministry because it will give him a place of influence.

His position will open to him the "best
homes," introduce him to congenial social life,
enable him to cultivate his taste for literature
and art, and insure a reserved seat in the synagogue of the honored of men.

Whenever any young man is approached in
this manner, he should ask his solicitor to lay
aside his robe, and he may then recognize
Satan clothed as an angel of light.

Not one crumb of comfort did Jesus leave
for the minister who seeks honor or chief place
in His kingdom. One can not but raise a question as to how many "great preachers" will be
seated at the right and left hand, respectively,
of our Lord, when heaven's banquet table is
spread in honor of those whom God delights
to recognize as "great." It is more than possi-

ble that when the King rises to introduce the guest of honor, He will name some one who labored in a stony field, where harvest was scant, and whose blistered hands hold merely the dropped gleanings of the "outstanding men." Down deep do we not heartily hope that will be the case?

After all, is it not the humble, patient toiler whom we really love? Perhaps the best loved ministers, both by God and man, are some whose fame has never spread beyond their local parishes.

If the Jerusalem widow really gave more than any other contributor when she shyly dropped her two mites, destined to become the most famous offering ever made, is it not highly probable that some unknown minister, perhaps not overly popular with his "superiors," will receive the degree: "MINISTER" (*summa cum laude*) at heaven's Commencement?

Another striking saying of Jesus to His ministers was, "Behold, I send you forth as sheep in the midst of wolves."

This does not indicate that the minister is to hold a very commanding position in affairs of this world. Wolves do not elect a sheep as pack leader, nor do they take orders from a lamb.

It is feared that in too many instances, in our educating and training of men for the ministry, we have come perilously near preparing them for that sort of religious leadership which professionalism has created. Religious professionalism damns the soul. Unable to use the language of the people, it speaks a strange tongue of its own creation, not the simple speech of servants, and heaven itself needs an interpreter to understand it, at times. "From this peril, good Lord, deliver us."

It is the survival of the priestly conception of ministering, a curse to the church during eighteen centuries. Eternal vigilance alone can protect even a people religiously democratic from the encroachment and enslavement of "clericalism." That system hangs many millstones about the necks of Christ's little ones. Religious Pharisaism, by "climbing up some other way," enters pulpits in the persons of clerically-minded preachers, and the flock suffers from its ravages.

Emphasis on this phase of ministerial temptation is justified, because of the fact that no other calling subjects men to such subtle temptations to spiritual pride.

It was spiritual pride that fathered the jealousy and lust for religious control which crucified Jesus.

Another sobering and informing generalization on the conception of ministering held by Jesus is found in **Matt. 16: 25, 26:** "For whosoever would save his life shall lose it: and whosoever shall lose his life for my sake shall find it. For what shall it profit a man if he gain the whole world and forfeit his life?"

A man's "world" is that area in which he lives, where his interests are, in which his goals are to be found. If, to gain his life objectives, he bankrupts his spiritual life, he loses all. Even ministers have done that. Some years ago, a man, long prominent in religious affairs, holding one of the most famous pulpits, preaching to hundreds weekly, came out before his public with a confession that, to gain the popularity he held, to attain the position of influence then his, he had neglected the inner spiritual life, had lowered the standards for membership in order to reach more people, and been more absorbed in building an "institution" than in encouraging regeneration. In short, to become famous as a "great preacher" he had bargained his soul for popularity and success. It was a pathetic story he told. His achievements had elevated him to the pinnacle of ministerial success, but his own evaluation of them was that they were "hay and stubble" structures. Ambition had led him to covet high position and had bred a superiority complex of which he felt profoundly ashamed late in life.

He who catches Jesus' meaning as to "saving and losing life" will crucify ambition so that aspiration will live in its place.

To the minister with a truly consecrated spirit, there is no "menial place," no "small field"; wherever he finds himself he will be happy in serving to the limit of his ability.

He has developed a "ministering complex" instead of a "superiority" one. The insignia for Christ's own minister should be the basin and towel, not a theological gown, not a bishop's miter, not key or scepter.

The "ministering" motive compels him to center his thought on what sinful men *are,* and work and pray that they may become new creatures.

When Jesus asked James and John if they could drink His cup and be baptized with His baptism, they envisioned a cup of joy and plenty, and a baptism of initiation into ecclesiastical rule and authority. Like the politician, about to have office "thrust upon him by the people," they unhesitatingly adjudged themselves "able." There must have been a break in Jesus' voice as He went on: "Ye shall indeed drink my cup and be baptized with my baptism." He knew the spiritual death and resurrection in their souls which must precede—how hard, how humbling, how disappointing it would be to them! But they were not truly great men till they drank His cup, with Him.

Like his Lord, the minister must "give his life" if many are to be ransomed through his ministering. He must insist on serving others more than on having them serve him.

It is well to close this chapter with a reference to the reassuring incident recorded in **John 20: 19-23.**

Jesus had suddenly appeared, become visible, in a group of agitated and disheartened preachers. One wonders also whether they were not embittered. Their Teacher and Lord, whom they had sworn never to deny, and whom they had hoped to see drive Pilate from his judgment hall, and Caiaphas from the presiding officer's seat in the Sanhedrin, had, at the orders of these rulers, unresistingly placed His shoulder under a cross, walked submissively to Calvary and died there in a few hours, as if He had lost all desire to live. Yet it was HE that they had hoped should redeem Israel! It looked as if He had failed them. That, they were in no frame of mind to forgive.

They were filled with fear, and fearful hearts are always troubled hearts.

They had been called to preach, had gone forth on a trial tour, returned exultingly, "Even the demons are subject to us in thy name." Success had made them jubilant. They still have that same urge to preach, but now they have no message. No more of a message than our pitiable intellectuals of today whose "wisdom" has crowded out faith, and have no better Christ to proclaim than that He was a unique Jewish teacher with a burning passion for social reform! No preacher need expect a ministry either happy or fruitful when he has permitted his divine Lord to be transmuted into a frail mortal by the alchemy of speculative skepticism.

To this despondent company of ten, Jesus, seemingly coming out of nowhere, stands before them and salutes with gracious courtesy, in Oriental phrase, "Peace be unto you! Peace be unto you!" Whence had He come? Doors were shut. He did not enter, He "appeared," as it would seem He always did after the resurrection. Despair yields to rapturous joy. Though their Lord had died, yet He is not dead! He symbolically clothes them with certain authority by breathing on them, promises the Spirit, renews their commission to preach, gives them a message of forgiveness for human sin. Peace would be theirs by faithful proclamation of that promise of forgiveness. Nothing but the assurance that His message can and will lead to forgiveness of sin can induce the dove of spiritual peace to settle in a true minister's heart. There are two essentials, at least, to a happy, contented, fruitful ministry. They are both suggested in this incident:

First, a positive conviction that the Person whom he proclaims is nothing less than the Christ, the Son of the Living God, with all the connotations of Deity which those words contain. This faith sustains in trial, strengthens in weakness, turns feebleness into power, comforts in sorrow, nerves for every conflict with sin.

Without such a Christ, it is difficult to understand how any minister could have "peace." At best, he is shadowed by uncertainty, and that is a disturbing, not peace-conferring, state of mind.

Second, an assurance, a consciousness, of having been "sent," guided by this Person, even as the Father had sent Him. He knows he will never be alone, for Jesus' appearances seem to have been timed to bring assurance to His disciples of His abiding presence. Whatever men may do or say about his ministry, he knows his Lord is with him, and understands

his need. This brings peace. Jesus is living.
He is with His minister. The belief of that
clearly demonstrable fact gives His servants
that "peace of God which passeth understanding."

Christ's minister must remember that his
mission is like his Master's in objective, not
in "having authority," nor with miraculous
power, but in seeking to save the lost by that
very gospel which has always been the power
of God unto salvation.

CHAPTER III

Terms Which Describe Ministering

A thorough study of all phases of ministering as found in the New Testament necessitates a careful look at the various words used in referring to those services. Both their etymology and current use will be illuminating and helpful for our purpose.

The word most frequently translated "minister" is the Greek word *diakonos,* from the verb *diakoneo.* It means "to serve; to act as deacon." The noun is defined, "One who executes the commands of another, especially of a master; a servant, attendant, minister." It refers to the *activity* of a servant in his work rather than to his relationship to his master as an inferior to a superior, although that status is clearly implied. It emphasizes *service* rather more than *servility.* As a general term, it denotes those through whom God carries on His administration of such activities among men as He desires to control. It describes a subordinate position in which certain active duties are to be performed.

It has been seen that Jesus placed the office of "minister" or "deacon" at the climactic official position in His kingdom. "He that would be great among you, let him be servant [minister] of all." And Jesus evidently meant just what those words imply—the minister is to serve *all* the congregation, in every capacity where he can do the work better than another, not any special class or group.

First reference to it as a place of preferment in the Jerusalem church is in **Acts 6: 2,** in connection with the choice of seven men to supervise the daily distribution of funds from the common treasury of those who had entered into a voluntary communism.

The apostles, appealed to for intervention in the disputes arising from charges of favoritism or neglect in deciding what the daily stipend should be for certain beneficiaries, refused to "turn aside to serve tables," but advised the selection of seven capable and trustworthy men to have charge of the matter. This arrangement would leave them free to give full time to preaching the Word, unencumbered with relief details. The men chosen by the congregation for this work were called "deacons" or "ministers."

Had our translators used one word instead of two in their rendering of this word *diakonos,* some confusion would have been avoided. The term "servant" is usually selected where a general or entirely unofficial position is referred to, and that is a proper distinction to make, perhaps. But there seems to be no sufficient reason for discrimination between a "minister" and a "deacon" ordinarily, except to give variety of expression. The conception which always underlies the use of the word is that an inferior is executing the will of a superior. It is a humble, but divinely approved word.

It may be affirmed with some confidence that it refers to a "ministry" in connection with the preaching of the gospel, not apart from it. It is not surprising, therefore, that some of the original seven "deacons" became successful preachers, as in the cases of Philip and Stephen.

Jesus describes His own mission to earth by selecting that word. In **Matt. 20:28** He says, "Even the Son of man came not to be ministered unto, but to minister, and to give his life a ransom for many." Paul, notwithstanding a vigorous defense of his rightful claim to the apostolate, often used the humble word "minister" both for himself and his fellow preachers. The fact is that much of the genius of Christianity is revealed in that word.

The minister is a subordinate: first, to Christ as Lord and Master; second, to the congregation. His special calling is to preach because, presumably, he can do that better than any other in the group. But that does not relieve him of other responsibilities which he can meet in a superior fashion. As servant of the church which supports him, he owes it all his time and talent, for both preaching the gospel and advancing the spiritual life and interests of the congregation in every possible manner.

One thing is certain: the true minister of Christ is never a boss or dictator in the church he serves. He may be, must be, a leader who commands a following among the people; not because of his "official position," but because his knowledge, wisdom, consecration, diligence in work, loyalty to Christ, and ability to do the things necessary to the success of the church. He must do his "ruling," if any, by the sheer force of his ministerial personality.

Another word used to describe ministering is *leitourgeo*. Etymologically, it denoted a service rendered to the Greek state, especially where one served at his own charges.

It had a patriotic flavor, since it was often used when referring to a political orator, a sort of "dollar-a-year-man," who took pains to work for civic betterment and progress, without thought of personal gain or office. It is rich in its suggestiveness of an undivided loyalty to the higher interests of an entire group. An illustration of the delicacy and tact which characterized the ministry of Paul is bound up in this word. In **Rom. 15: 16,** writing to Gentiles, people unaccustomed to make contributions for spiritual benefits received, he says, "I was made a *leitourgos* to the Gentiles." That emphasized the fact that he was neither seeking nor expecting material help from them. He counted it a joy to "serve at his own charges." He felt a justifiable pride in having been called by Christ for the most unselfish type of ministerial labor that fell to the apostolic lot. When Jesus selected him for Gentile territory, doubtless one reason was that Paul, a tent maker, could find remunerative employment easily in those regions where so many nomadic folk lived or traded.

Another word, *uperetes,* presents a somewhat different phase of ministering. It means, literally, "an under rower, a subordinate rower"; that is, one of the lowliest among the lowly.

That was the position assigned to the lowest galley slaves. Jesus used this word in **Acts**

22:15, when He appeared to Paul on the Damascus road, to qualify him to be an apostle. He frankly informed the proud Pharisee that his days of influence and power among Sanhedrists was at an end, if he accepted the challenge of this call. Never again could he start on a trip "with authority from the chief priests" to make arrests. He would find himself among the lowly, often in bonds. The immediate and elated response of the apostle to the Gentiles, revealed the wisdom of Jesus in the selection. In spite of the earlier years of persecuting zeal, Paul had much in common with his Lord. Neither of them ever invited men to follow Christ for gain, prestige, office, power. Both taught that the way would be narrow. They rejoiced to walk in it themselves, and appealed only to those souls heroic enough to share hardships with them. Paul knew the death Jesus had died, and when He appeared in the glorified state, Paul saw that the way to the crown was that of the cross, and deliberately took it.

Luke (**Luke 1:2**) acknowledges these "under rowers," along with others as eyewitnesses, and sources for his material when writing his Gospel. This is a tribute to the reliability of the testimony of the first "ministers" who served in obscurity. No author mentions sources of knowledge consulted by him, if they were of doubted veracity. The fact that Luke includes them in his bibliography list is sufficient evidence that they were held in high esteem by those outside the church as well as those inside it, for he wrote to convince unbelievers that Jesus was the Christ.

Our study is making it increasingly evident that true "ministers" rank high with Christ but low with men. Fortunate that preacher who does not reverse that order for himself.

The hardest, but most blessed, word of all used to denote the work of the ministry, is *doulos* or "slave."

It was Paul's favorite title for himself. He merited a high academic degree, doubtless, but he preferred "slave," and wrote it after his name with Christian pride. It emphasized the fact that he had not the liberty to do or teach as he pleased. He had died and Christ lived in him, therefore he must do the will of Him who had supplanted self. He was "not his own." He had "been bought with a price." No other station in life is so blessed as that of being the slave of a divine Master. All one need do is to execute the will of his Lord. The Master assumes all responsibility and all authority for activities and results, including rewards. The slave merely obeys, knowing it is to the interest of the Master to care for him.

Such a servant will not become the servant of
sin, nor of ecclesiastical machines. The spiritual rulers of this world will have no terror
for him. He has a Master in heaven, above
any and all earthly authorities. His sense of
security in spiritual things will lessen his
anxiety concerning security in material things.
None but such a slave can be really free.

None but those so enslaved to Christ can
fulfill life's mission.

Those made in the image of God should
act in Godlike living as God's own Son acted,
viz., in subjecting all things to the Father.
That leaves no room for personal liberty, save
the liberty to do that which pleases God. This
relationship of the minister to Christ as His
slave, deserves a volume on ministerial functions.

We now pass to a group of words in which
the thought of "preaching" is prominent.

The one most frequently used is *euange-
lidzo*.

It is defined, "To bring good news, to
announce glad tidings." Our word "gospel"
is its best translation. Jewish thought, in the
first Christian century, was centered largely
around the "good news" which the Messianic
hope engendered. The word "gospel," therefore, had in it more than veiled Messianic

expectation. It qualified the nature of that hope as good, desirable, comforting. It must have been the finest word of the day in religious circles. It seems to have been connected indissolubly with the prophetic desires and predictions of the Old Testament. Simeon's devout wish to be gathered to his fathers after his eyes had seen "the consolation of Israel," at the time of Jesus' presentation in the temple, indicated that he believed this gospel could redeem his people. That was indeed "good tidings" to him. It was also "news" at that time. The element of joy in the gospel should never be overlooked. Joy in the heart of the forgiven sinner. Joy among men. Joy in heaven. God the Father, Christ the Son, the Holy Spirit the convicting Comforter, all shared, continue to share, that joy. What an abundance of holy joy is in store for the loyal gospel preacher! When a man is not happy in his ministry, there is something radically wrong. If a minister of Christ does not find that joy early in his labors, perhaps he has erred in his choice, and should seek another area of endeavor. Without that joy, a sense of frustration will becloud the preacher's life, and no one else is quite so pitiable as the preacher who drinks himself drunk at the poison fountain of defeatism. God may follow

him for a time, even prepare providential food
for him as He did for Elijah in his wilderness
flight.   But unless his spirit is revived, he
should be courageous enough to anoint some
Elisha in his stead—and wait for heaven's
whirlwind.

Where the thought of public announcement, by means of a proclamation, or declaration with emphasis, is to be conveyed, the word
kataggelo, is used several times.

There is in it the suggestion of a message
from a higher to a lower, that is, from one in
authority to one under authority.   This is the
word Luke uses in his account of the preaching
of Saul and Barnabas at Salamis, as they began
their missionary labors.   It carries an idea of
thoroughness or *completeness*.   It is of a
preacher who so proclaims the gospel that Paul,
in **1 Cor. 9:14,** declares that "they who preach
the gospel should live of the gospel."   It is
not straining an etymological point to infer,
if Paul's choice of term was not accidental or
purposeless, that the preacher who deletes anything from the gospel message as proclaimed
by inspired men, who soft-pedal portions of it,
who serves with a divided interest, or is unqual-
ified to proclaim it adequately, holds no genuine
claim to ministerial support.   The apostle
scarcely meant that every man who decided

that he would preach was entitled to be housed and fed merely by virtue of his self-appointed task.

Another interesting word used to describe the preaching of the first Christians is *diaggelo*. It means "To carry a message through; announce everywhere, through places, through assemblies; to publish abroad; to declare," etc. The territorial expansion of the preaching mission is a central thought in it. Jesus used this word when He gave His curt and stinging rebuke to the hesitant, would-be disciple, who asked permission to delay public acknowledgment of Christ as Lord, till after his father had died—probably to avoid family alienations and disinheritance.

The timorous man was given a hard order. Instead of waiting till hindrances disappeared of themselves, Jesus ordered "Let the dead bury their own dead; but go thou and publish abroad the kingdom of God." He was commanded to "proclaim thoroughly, everywhere, in various groups," his discipleship. Let us hope he obeyed. One who has made great personal sacrifice for Christ becomes a desirable object lesson of courage and conviction, two essentials in discipleship, always. The timid preacher, seeking the path where the going is easy, overanxious to avoid opposition by friends or foes of his Lord, should study the incident cited above.

Several times Luke uses a very descriptive word in his record of Paul's preaching, especially in the synagogues. It is *dialegomai*. It means "To think different things with one's self, mingle thought with thought, to ponder, revolve in mind," etc. A fitting translation for it, often, is "to reason." Luke states that Paul "reasoned" with his brethren in the synagogues. This word supplies Scriptural authority for religious debate, comparison of views, etc., where the discovery of truth is the object. Very often convincing testimony or argument relative to the claims of Christ must be presented by this method.

Perhaps no more suggestive word for preaching can be used then *kerusso*, "to preach." John the Baptist came "preaching; Jesus Himself "preached"; He sent the twelve out to "preach"; Philip and Paul "preached." Literally, all these were "heralds" of the gospel message, that being the meaning of the word under scrutiny. The "herald" summoned the contestants to the games. He proclaimed the approach of rulers. He announced royal decrees. He always spoke "with a suggestion of formality, gravity, and an authority which must be listened to and obeyed."

He was a duly accredited proclaimer, announcer, of the message or decree of a superior. A "herald" was chosen because of his understanding of the importance of the news or summons he announced, his ability to repeat it intelligently and his fidelity to the trust committed to him. Often his message was a legal proclamation, and should be delivered in the very words of the official document itself. He was the voice of the authority which commissioned him, as John the Baptist asserted for himself when asked who he was. "I am the voice," or vocal messenger of Him who was to come. No liberty as to message content was his. He dare not alter it to suit the people to whom it was delivered. No word or paragraph could be omitted. Nothing could be added.

The voice of the herald is a voice from the throne of heaven's King. He is only a "voice," not a legislator, not an executive, not a judge. A preacher who is deeply sensitive of the authority of the message he delivers should think seriously of his "heralding." Not only were "those who contend in the games to contend lawfully," but they must be summoned to the contest by a lawfully accredited "herald," and advised of the rules governing the contest.

The "herald of the gospel" has a responsible task.

The favorite word, however, used to designate the work of ministering, both publicly and privately, is *didaskalos*. It means "teacher." Jesus named His followers "disciples," or pupils in His school. Later, after they had been trained by Him, they were sent out as "teachers." Teacher (rabbi) was the title usually employed in addressing Him by both friends and enemies, and Jesus never rebuked them for it. He accepted the honor implied as merited. He was responsible for both the curriculum and training of His disciples. He spoke with authority, and as they mastered His teachings, they boldly proclaimed the same doctrines, quoting Jesus as their authority.

Jesus personally taught the men whom He entrusted to teach others the principles and commandments of His gospel. The good seed of the kingdom was to be sowed by teaching. Jesus had no alternative method. It is frequently asserted that example is the best method of teaching the Christian faith. This statement, like partial truth generally, is deceptive and perilous. Christian morality is the fruit of the Christian faith, but it is not the faith itself. Faith is an intellectual and moral judgment based on credible testimony, and testimony is presented by teaching. In the Book of Acts, teaching is almost always synonymous with preaching, that phase of ministering being referred to some forty times. Emphasis on teaching abounds in the Epistles. When Paul wrote to Timothy, he cited his own example as a teacher in exhorting his son in the gospel to give heed to his teaching. Upon his final leave-taking of the Ephesian elders, Paul reminded them that he had taught publicly and from house to house for three years. The public teaching was by sermon. The "house to house" teaching must have been what we know as "personal work," or individual instruction.

The writer of Hebrews deplores the slow development of "teachers" in the church. This indicates that all, ministers and members, were expected to be qualified to teach. The Jerusalem church grew so rapidly at first because it had a large number of teachers.

The importance of instructional work in the church cannot be overemphasized. All successful kingdom building depends upon accurate and loyal teaching, for which the New Testament provides all the necessary curricular content. A building preacher must be a teaching preacher. A strong church must be an intelligent church.

And it must be intelligent in the New Testament teaching if it is to be a truly spiritual institution. The first missionary enterprise on record which was sponsored by a single congregation was that undertaken by the church at Antioch in Syria, where "prophets and teachers" were numerous. The missionary passion flames brightest in the breast of the teaching missionary. It does more than illuminate, it consumes dross and causes love to glow. The missionary achievements of the past century were invariably in direct ratio to the emphasis on Scriptural teaching in the Bible schools. So long as the Bible was accepted as a book of divine authority in religion, its teachers had a message for which they could afford to die, and their teaching was with convincing power. When other emphases supplanted Biblical teaching, missions, philanthropy, benevolences and conversions decreased in direct ratio to the stress placed on the substitutionary curricula. It is worth repeating: the church-building preacher must be a teaching preacher.

Despite its triteness, it must be said: the teaching preacher must be intelligent. Intelligence results from hard work. It is not a direct gift from God. Ability to comprehend, facility of speech, etc., may be natural endowments. But knowledge of the Word of God is a possession of the student only. The preacher, therefore, can not please his Lord, his congregation, or himself, unless he is a hard worker. Paul looked on the work of a teaching elder as laborious. "Faithful is the saying, if a man seeketh the office of a bishop, he seeketh a *good work*" (**1 Tim. 3:1**). All "good work" is hard work. Ministers, faithful to their trusts, cannot hope to be carried to the skies on flowery beds of ease. They may be, let us hope they will be, carried to the cemetery in that fashion; but never to a place of high esteem on the part of God or man, if they are at ease in Zion. The minister should be the busiest man in the church, but he should also be careful about *what* he is busy. It is not sufficient that he work hard; he must work hard at the right thing.

He may be as industrious as Solomon's ant in "serving" folk and interests to the neglect of his ministerial responsibility.

A thousand askings will come for addresses at every sort of function—business, political, social, educational, community enterprises, even athletic and recreational activities. He is often sought because his services may be had without cost, and he is tempted to respond from a sense of community obligation. Should he yield to such importunities frequently, he will have little time for his own work. Outside demands will increase to the point where he is a mere errand boy or community factotum. He may mistake the applause of those using him as indicative of growing influence and enlarged constituency, only to discover too late that the folk who support him that he may devote his time to ministering to the spiritual welfare of the congregation deem his usefulness at an end, and they grant him a six-month leave of absence, renewable twice a year.

Not only so, but many good ministers have learned to their sorrow that various organizations have sought their ministerial influence and personal services to camouflage certain ulterior purposes for which the organization came into being. Too often ministerial respectability has been compromised by being identified with a disreputable enterprise masquerading as a religious or reform organization. High-minded and public-spirited preachers are especially susceptible to the wiles designing promoters usually employ.

The heart-breaking disillusionment suffered by a number of men who became involved in the intrigues of a certain alliterative organization of the third decade of this century may be cited as an example. So long as it could use the preacher as a tool in promoting its political and personal ambitions, it was "very religious." Once its ends gained, the church whose favor it had sought was contemptuously ignored. Before being lured from his supreme work of preaching the gospel, the minister should be absolutely sure that Jesus Himself would approve such diversion of his energies.

The successful teaching preacher must, *simply must,* spend much time in his study. That is the inner sanctuary of his worklife. It should be holy ground to him. Leaving his shoes of worldly ambition and pollution outside, let him enter in barefoot humility, pausing in the "closet" to pray for the help of God in preparing a message that will exalt the Christ. Childlike faith and Paul-like devotion should breathe through every sermon. Anything less than this spirit is unworthy. The preacher owes the congregation he serves the very best of which he is capable in his sermonic productions. His study habits are therefore important. While he is delivering a thirty-minute sermon, an audience of five or six hundred people will be giving him almost a month of their combined daily working time. Unless his message is the best he can produce, he should feel himself guilty of moral embezzlement or spiritual banditry in robbing them of

precious hours. The hold-up man uses a loaded
gun in his work, and takes mere filthy lucre
which the victim may replace. The lazy and
unprepared preacher uses his mouth only in
"holding up" his audience, and takes their
valuable time which even God Himself can
never restore to them. None but a studious
man can deliver a sermon that is Scriptural
and apt. A scholarly (not stilted or pedantic)
ministry is more likely to be long and profitable. It takes a congregation a long time to
tire of a man who really ministers in "word
and doctrine," and in deed. "Congregational
restlessness and fickleness" are not the only
things that load a moving van for a preacher.
The indolent, disinterested or worldly preacher
often rides in one when he should be in a spiritual hearse. Paul's exhortation to Timothy to
"study to show thyself a workman that needeth
not to be ashamed, rightly dividing the word
of truth," was possibly fatherly advice from
the older man who feared that his son in the
gospel might become too deeply engrossed in
petty details in ministering, or content to carry
the dead laurel wreaths of former victories.
The preacher should never permit a medal of
achievement to be pinned on him while living.
After he is dead if someone insists on it, perhaps he will not be so flattered by it as to go

strutting through heaven displaying it on his robe! He should never feel that he has "attained," but is always "pressing forward toward" his best, which is ever a little in advance of what he now is. As he reaches that period when the outward man is decaying, very often he may watch the inward man being renewed day by day. Exceptional men have graced the pulpit, and delighted the devout pew, after three score and ten. It was because they refused to die at the top. One is tempted to believe that most of us set the day of our intellectual and spiritual demise. A life of vigor in the realm of ministerial service may be prolonged by sheer determination, barring the entrance of senility by strenuous effort to make tomorrow better than today.

There is decided value in having fixed study habits and hours. The schedule will be broken frequently, of necessity; but a schedule there should be. It is said that Jowett had a special chair in which he sat, placed in a certain corner of his study, when he composed his sermons. He felt it impossible to do his best work in any other place. Perhaps not every preacher is so sensitive to custom or environment. In fact, he should not be a slave to external things. But a well-grooved habit in study reduces the friction of conscious effort in concentration. His sermonic work should be done with some attention to routine, to prevent the dissipation of thought, which unusual experiences encourage.

No man has a better opportunity, or a greater temptation, to become lazy and flabby in intellectual fiber. His time is largely his own. He punches no time clock. Seldom is he questioned concerning his activities. He is trusted by the congregation to use all his time in building the local church, and he ought to have a keen conscience on the matter of keeping that trust sacred.

Desultory habits may creep on him unawares. He may degenerate from a student to a casual reader of printed material and relay what he reads without having investigated its truth or weighed its worth. Much "heterodoxy" would have been avoided if ministers had thought to themselves instead of "out loud." It is seriously immoral for a preacher to proclaim some theory or doctrine merely because it has made a favorable impression on him when first read. Of all men, he should be the most skeptical about so-called human wisdom where it runs counter to God's revelations. He must remember that the science of yesterday was considered as unassailable then as that of today is at present, and not hesitate to challenge anything that men hold as a theory which discredits the Book which is his text for teaching. But the careless reader and slovenly thinker is unable to put pretentious "wisdom" and "scholarly discoveries" on the stand for cross-examination. The minister ought to be the most independent thinker in the community. His religious truth has been revealed by the personified Truth, Him who said "I am the truth," and there is nothing to be added to that. He is responsible for explaining and applying the truth revealed, not for "discovering new truth." New uses, new aspects, new applications of that truth will be coming to him as he studies it; but not new truth.

It is unwise to hoard sermonic creations, if he can be tempted to repeat them on unsuspecting hearers. Some auditor may have a memory that will prove embarrassing, and such a hearer is the last one the preacher can afford to disappoint. Careful listeners have prevented more than one preacher from premature approach to the "dead line."

Truth is eternal, unchanging, but people become enthusiastic about it only when it is becomingly dressed. If the preacher never puts a new metaphorical suit on an idea, it soon loses its "crease" and is not "presentable." He may neglect his trousers, perhaps, with

impunity. Some great preachers even today
run the risk involved in that. But the sermon
must be "freshly pressed" with every appearance it makes in public. Patched and worn
clothes may be no disgrace to the minister, but
a shabby or badly patched sermon has "no forgiveness in this life nor that which is to come"!
This may not be the "unpardonable sin" about
which the minister preaches, but it will soon
be such to a discriminating congregation. "The
last state of that preacher will be worse than
the first."

The preacher needs a *Bible in his study*.
This observation is made because many deliverances which pass for sermons today give no
evidence that such a book is in the "sanctum."
The *ipse dixit* of the preacher is substituted
for a "thus saith the Lord." He can escape
censure for his discourteous refusal to acknowledge any acquaintance with the Bible, introducing as his proof-texts the inane or pedantic
utterances of pulpiteers or philosophers on whom
the spotlight happens to be turned just now,
because so few of his hearers neither know
nor care whether he quotes Paul or Gandhi.
The lack of Biblical preaching in recent years
has led to shameful ignorance of the Bible
itself. But the need for its truth is even
greater because of that fact. It is not an over-

statement to say that the minister should devote more time to study of, and meditation on, the Bible than on all other writings he may possess. Not so much what other men have written about it; not too slavish a use of commentaries; but an independent, personal study of it.

The Bible is God's calling card and letter of introduction to our race. It tells who He is, announces His purposes, declares His program, reveals His motives, records His commands, contains His warnings and pledges His rewards for the faithful doing of His will.

Biblical preaching will stimulate at least some interest in Bible reading. It will enable its readers to be intelligent in their applications of its truths. In the process of reconstructing the background out of which the inspired writings came, the Biblical preacher will find sermon suggestions leaping at him from every page. To his amazement and delight, he will discover that the Bible itself furnishes a setting for the discussion of every real need of the human heart today, as it did in the day it was written. The preaching of sermons thus born will insure originality and will edify the hearers. The contemporaneousness of the Bible with today's best thought is worthy of a volume. It is a newer book than those not yet written about it. The most refreshing and inspiring preacher is the Bible preacher. Ere he becomes conscious of it himself, his hearers will be remarking about the value of his "expositions"—perhaps the highest type of sermonic deliverances in any age. The Bible-saturated sermon, provided it be not mere parroting of Biblical phraseology without regard to its fittingness, is never a dull one. Auditors neither slumber nor sleep during its delivery.

If the young men now in training for the ministry could only realize the importance of such preaching, understand how hungry people are for it, know what a dearth of it there has been in the past decades, they would go forth to create a new place for the church and its Head in the planning of men. Bible colleges and seminaries owe it to the churches and individuals supporting them to prepare their students for Bible preaching.

The leanness of recent years in spiritual living, so deplored by all religious groups, is easily accounted for. The harvests of the years full of spiritual power, because of emphasis on the Bible as a divine revelation, have been consumed. A large share of the responsibility for the present status must be assumed by professional religious training schools. Not that all of them are equally guilty. They are not. God be thanked for a considerable number which have not bowed the knee to modern educational "baals." (One almost wishes for a "b" smaller than the lower case type with which to write that word "baal.") A most encouraging fact is that those colleges in which devout Biblical study is still made the major requirement in ministerial preparation, are training perhaps 75 per cent of our future preachers. Those schools and churches that have yielded to the temptation to go "modern" for the loaves and fishes of popular approval, are sterile. Not one of them is reproducing. No alarm need be felt about that fact. It is no indictment of nature that hybrids are so often sterile. A hybrid Christianity and agnostic philosophy is scarcely worth perpetuating.

It is difficult to see why so much importance is attached to certain curricular requirements in many schools established to prepare young men for a successful ministry. Just why should students be led on exploring expeditions through deserts of critical theories *about* the Bible, and the Biblical text itself remain an unknown region to them? The guides provided for such expeditions are usually merely a clannish group of spiritual nomads who are resentful of the restrictions imposed on doctrine and life by a volume that claims to have proceeded from the Spirit of God.

For diversion, these neophytes may be turned over to the speculative educational philosopher for a trip into certain "experience-centered" swamps in a search for cultural, ethical or spiritual "controls."

After a few years of meanderings in such barren wastes, is it strange that the young minister emerges to face the practical tasks his calling imposes, confused or bewildered? He immediately begins to deal with people who are harassed by the vexations of everyday life. They are beset by temptations both blatant and subtle. Many of them are worried with anxiety about the morrow. Into some of the homes connected with the church, tragedies which challenge faith have forced entrance. People are asking bread, and he discovers nothing but stones in his basket. They clamor for assurance, and he can offer only a probability. They want a rock on which to build their hopes, but he discovers he has been trained in kindergarten sand construction, and wonders whether real rock exists. He sympathizes with them, but can not understand their grand hailing sign of distress. Perhaps, in his despair, he may be induced to turn to the neglected Book to see what others in former ages found in it, and find both the message he is seeking, and himself. Every man can find himself in the Bible, even the preacher being no exception. No good reason for being "lost" exists today.

At the risk of criticism for repetitive statements, in the light of present need and the failure of everything else to produce ministers who can build local congregations, emphasis is once more given to the imperative demand for a "teaching ministry" which majors on teaching the Bible. This Book should either be made the only textbook for Christian education and taught as the revelation from God to man, or repudiated in its entirety. Upon the restoration of the Bible to its rightful place in ministerial study courses depends the future of Christianity.

Returning to the discussion of the minister in his study, the proper use of sermons by other preachers of sermonic ability is suggested. Without raising the question of plagiaristic sin, the unwisdom of copying other men's sermons will be conceded.

Better to preach in a mail-order store suit, made for some man several sizes removed from the wearer, than to parade a homiletic creation of a greater preacher, without duly warning the congregation of what to expect. Sermons should be studied, not copied.

All sermons worth one's while to read will be found to be the pen product of men who

believe in Jesus as the Christ and the Bible
as an inspired book of authority. The young
man who really wants to preach the gospel
will find it a disappointing waste of time to
read the vapid meanderings of a philosophic
guess, masquerading as a sermonic discovery.
Sermons profitable for use in the study, are
products of a tried faith, tested and found not
wanting. They may have been born out of
travail of soul over some parishioner, or some
sinner whom he would win. Christ's greatest
preacher wrote, "My little children, of whom
I am again in travail until Christ be formed
in you"—and broke at that very point in his
letter to wipe the tears from his eyes—never
finishing the sentence. But the sob of the
sermon was transcribed to the parchment on
which he wrote, and sermons originating in
that kind of emotion are convincing. Many
godly men have left specimens of that sort of
sermonizing, and their study is always profitable. Sermons that glow with a chastened
love, that flame with passionate fire in defense
of the gospel and its Author, that comfort
broken hearts, that truly instruct in the way
of salvation, that undergird a weakening faith,
that lead to man's reconciliation with God and
his fellow-man, that buoy a struggling soul
with the hope of eternal life, that can turn

lamentations of defeat into shouts of victory—
these are worth the time of the minister in
his study.

Much other reading matter should find its
way into the study. Biographies of great men,
preachers and non-preachers, in addition to
their broadening and educational value, will
provide a thesaurus of illustrative material.
They are especially valuable in their revelation
of the unchanging character of human nature.

Well-written biographies lead an interesting
procession of redeemed and unredeemed men
before the reader in panoramic march.

They add greatly to one's understanding of
the folk he wants to serve, justifying their
place in the minister's library.

Since it is important that the preacher keep
a little ahead of the thinking of the people to
whom he ministers, so far as time and purse
permit, he should avail himself of the use of
preachers' magazines and religious journals,
of current literature with informing or literary
merit, together with books covering a wide
range of subject matter. If all this suggests
a rather large order, remember that ministering
itself is a large order!

The study program of the minister, however, dare not be confined to his "study" or
library. He must know how to read the "living

literature" in the midst of whom he mingles daily. He must know people and their needs. Men and women and children provide postgraduate courses which he never quite completes.

Were there no other reasons for pastoral visitation, the minister should see the people among whom he serves in their homes, to learn what they really are, and determine what they may become.

A single call will not suffice for that. But after he has been with them in seasons of joy: at their weddings; family reunions; the first days in a new home; when babies come to brighten life; when promotion and graduation days are celebrated by their youth; when some honor has been bestowed on the family, etc., he will see whether happy experiences help or hinder the growth of a truly spiritual life.

After he has shared with them in sorrow: when serious illness of one beloved in the home has occasioned sleepless anxiety; when death invades; when misunderstandings arise and jealousies divide; when domestic troubles threaten the foundation of the home; when griefs deeper than those caused by death tear hearts; when earthly possessions are all lost—another side of the life of those whom he would help is revealed. Unless he has shared with them the whole gamut of spiritual experiences, he can not really know them.

This is the hardest, the most exhausting, the most nerve-depleting work on the minister's schedule. But it must be faithfully, cheerfully, prayerfully done.

In all this work, he is the one trusted by the congregation as their representative in service, one to another. He is the church's living expression of brotherly love and sympathetic ministration. It is a great honor, a sobering trust.

CHAPTER IV

Orders and Phases of Ministry

There is one paragraph in the New Testament which seems to epitomize the entire subject of ministering. It names the various orders or ranks of ministering servants and states the purpose of all such labor in the church. It reads like an abstract of Jesus' teaching to the twelve, outlining in chronological succession, the progress He desired to be made in building up His body, the church. That He had very definite plans for establishing and promoting His kingdom, is made crystal clear by this passage. A careful study of the ideal in ministering set forth therein should be fruitful.

The passage is found in **Eph. 4: 11-16:** "And he gave some to be apostles; and some, prophets; and some, evangelists; and some, pastors and teachers; for the perfecting of the saints, unto the work of ministering, unto the building up of the body of Christ: till we all attain unto the unity of the faith, and of the knowledge of the Son of God, unto a full-grown man, unto the measure of the stature of the fulness of Christ: that we may be no longer children, tossed to and fro and carried about with every wind of doctrine, by the sleight of men, in craftiness, after the wiles of error; but speaking truth in love, may grow up in all things unto him, who is the head, even Christ; from whom all the body fitly framed and knit together through that which every joint supplieth, according to the working in due measure of each several part, maketh the increase of the body unto the building up of itself in love."

Paul here gives first place in rank, as well as in authority, to the apostles. That concedes primacy in function to them. Power was theirs, delegated by Christ Himself to them personally, each one having been called individually. Matthew, in the tenth chapter of his gospel, has left a detailed account of Jesus' selection of the twelve, naming them, and specifying the nature of their enduement. Later, Paul was added. They are the most famous company of thirteen men earth has known.

Jesus named them "apostles," a word of Greek origin, meaning "a delegate, a messenger, one sent forth with orders." They were

Christ's first "missioners." Their trial assignment was " to the lost sheep of the house of
Israel." In that land, a sheep which had strayed
from the flock to which it belonged, was "lost."

It was careless or incompetent shepherding
that permitted sheep to stray. The properly
shepherded flock was always guarded, always
safe. It was just before selecting these men,
as Matthew records the event, that Jesus had
expressed a deep concern, had felt compassion
for the "multitude who were like sheep without
a shepherd." It was this compassion for lost
men that drove Him, by the compulsion of
infinite love, into the "form of a servant, being
made in the likeness of men" (**Phil. 2: 7**), that
He might shepherd all wandering humanity.
That simple declaration of His was a public
indictment of Israel's religious leadership. The
scribes and Pharisees and priests all carried
shepherds' staves and insisted upon exclusive
rights to care for the flock. Jesus boldly challenged their faithfulness when He characterized the sheep of Jehovah as shepherdless.
Keen observers might have forecast at that
very moment His untimely end, for ecclesias-
ticisms have never tolerated rebuke.

When they had received sufficient instruction, Jesus sent the twelve out on an experien-
tial itinerary. After this trial trip, they were

to report. He cautioned them to confine their labors to their own race, avoiding all Gentile and Samaritan territory.

Orders were given to "cast out demons, heal all manner of sickness, cleanse the lepers, raise the dead," the doing of which necessitated power to work miracles. Without divine endue-ment they could not have performed a single one of their assigned tasks. The "wonders and signs" wrought by them would assemble an audience, and accredit them as messengers of God.

The gospel message entrusted to them on this first ministry was an announcement. Upon the authority of Jesus, they were to proclaim "the kingdom of heaven is at hand." For the correct delivery of the message, the directing and controlling presence of the Holy Spirit was pledged, whenever need arose for His help. Because "the laborer is worthy of his hire," they were instructed to carry no expense money. The bounty of those to whom they ministered was to care for them. Though warned of dangers and persecutions, they were assured that their lives would be spared. Both their teaching and the ministrations they rendered were limited to the commission under which they went forth. It may not be amiss to assume that similar limitations should be recognized

by ministers today. Their responsibility begins
and ends with the commission given by Christ
Himself:

Later, a message of enlarged content was
entrusted to them. Shortly before His ascension, Jesus gave them the "Great Commission,"
in which all territorial, racial and cultural lines
were ignored (**Matt. 28: 18-20**). It was Jesus'
will that all, everywhere, should hear the same
"gospel," which was a call to faith in Jesus
as the Christ, the Son of the Living God, repentance from sin, confession before men of the
Lordship of Jesus Christ, and baptism into
His name, as conditional to the forgiveness of
sin and a restoration of lost fellowship with
God. The content of the term "gospel" includes
everything that is truly religious.

Before starting on the mission, they were
ordered to "tarry in Jerusalem until endued
with power from on high," by a "baptism in
the Holy Spirit." Obedient to this command-
ment, they waited until Pentecost, when the
promise of Holy Spirit enduement and guidance
was fulfilled. On that day, they "spake as the
Spirit gave them utterance," and through their
ministry on that day, the church came into
being. Three thousand obedient believers were
added to the nucleus remaining faithful after
Jesus' death.

That occasion was the beginning of their "witnessing" to the fact of Jesus' resurrection, the basic fact of His gospel.

None but personal eyewitnesses of Jesus, resurrected, could testify to that fact. To qualify Paul for the apostolate, Jesus appeared to him on the Damascan plain, and repeatedly manifested Himself to him later. In outlining the credentials which a successor to Judas must have, Peter, in connection with the selection of Matthias, insisted that he must have known Jesus personally during His ministry, be a witness to His death, and have accompanied with Him after His resurrection, up till the time of the ascension. This fact settles finally the question of "apostolic succession." It is impossible for any apostle to have a "successor," ecclesiastical word-juggling and textual manipulation to the contrary notwithstanding. This matter, like so many other disputed doctrines concerning the church, its duly authorized teachings, its ministries, etc., may be disposed of very simply by introducing New Testament testimony and permitting that to be final.

The promise Jesus made to Peter at Cæsarea Philippi, that the keys of the kingdom of heaven should be given to him; that whatsoever he bound on earth should be bound in heaven, and whatsoever he loosed on earth should be loosed in heaven, was afterward pledged to all apostles alike (**John 20: 21-23**). The identical language used in addressing Peter was used in addressing the twelve as a group. Peter therefore had no "primacy," unless the fact that his name heads each list of apostles might be so termed. No special message of authority, no peculiar ecclesiastical superiority, no earthly vice-gerency for Jesus, is even remotely hinted at in Jesus' dealings with Peter. The entire apostolic group were accredited equally as Jesus' messengers to men in sin. The "authority" given them was authority to "proclaim." The gospel they preached was "in the name of Christ," that is, with His authoritative sanction.

But administrative or ecclesiastical authority is not stated or implied in Jesus' promise of Holy Spirit guidance. When opportunity to exercise such authority stalked unbidden into their midst, as in the instance in which the Grecian Jews' complaint of neglect was brought to them for settlement, they refused to name men for even the lowly office of relief administration. They threw the matter right back into the congregation, saying, "Look you out from among you seven men of good report, full of the Spirit and of wisdom,

whom we may appoint over this business,"
that they might be free to execute their trust—
preaching, proclaiming, instructing, etc. They
participated in it only to the extent of giving
formal ratification to the choice made by the
congregation. They seem to have felt that
their authority was limited to the proclamation
of Christ's gospel for the forgiveness of sin,
and instruction to the new converts in the art
of Christian living. Those hearers who obeyed
their "gospel" were promised forgiveness, or,
"loosing" from their sins; those who refused
to obey were notified that they were unfor-
given, or, "bound" in their sins. It is perfectly clear to a discerning student of New
Testament teaching that those who see ecclesiastical content in Jesus' commission to the
twelve, behold only their own organizationally-
minded reflection in the pool of His truth. The
special office of apostle was to pass, along with
the special miraculous endowments of the Holy
Spirit, as Paul positively taught in **1 Corinthians 12, 13.**

Four varying but harmonious versions of
the "Great Commission" agree that Christly
authority was bestowed on the *message* the
apostles were sent to preach, not that official
authority was given to them to name successors
to their office. It will bear repetition: the only

authority conferred on the apostles was authority to preach, proclaim, teach, instruct in the gospel. The power granted to work miracles was to accredit a message, not to establish ecclesiastical claims. Had the latter been the purpose, every "successor" would have been empowered to demonstrate his office by similar miraculous gifts.

A word concerning the inclusion of Barnabas as an "apostle," along with Paul, in **Acts 14: 14** may be well. Both were "apostles" (or "missionaries," to use a modern word) of the church of Antioch, since it had sent them out with its blessing and probably provided expense money for the itinerary Barnabas was not "an apostle of Jesus Christ," such as Paul.

While not, strictly speaking, germane to the theme under discussion, it may be permissible to note that the promised help and guidance, or control, of the Holy Spirit, did not extend to their conduct. It was a *teaching* enduement. So far as their moral living or submission to Spirit leading was concerned, they had nothing that is not available to all today. They were not mere puppets. The authority carried in their teaching and writing was purely of an instructional character. We are not, therefore, justified in imitating them in life, save insofar as their conduct is an interpretation of the application of Jesus' ideals to doctrines and ordinances of the church. The baptism of the Holy Spirit did not insure their sinlessness. That Peter, at least, did "dissimulate" (a rather hard word, by the way, often spelled with three letters!) is Paul's charge in **Gal. 2: 11-21.**

We sometimes hear of an "approved precedent" cited as having apostolic origin and authority. There is such a thing. But it is to be found in the example or procedure of the apostles' work in executing Jesus' commands, not in their own personal conduct, in which human weakness may be detected occasionally.

The New Testament age had also specially endowed "prophets," seemingly invested with the power of "seers." They were colaborers with the apostles, usually found ministering to churches already established, whereas the apostles, like the evangelists, majored on the establishment of new congregations. This order of prophets disappeared with the passing of the apostolic age. An illustration of predictive knowledge on the part of one of them, named Agabus, is recorded in **Acts 11: 27-30; 21: 10.** He foretold a sore famine, and the brethren relied so confidently on his forecast that they began to prepare for it at once, raising funds for the relief of those who would be sufferers.

Prophets were also living at Antioch when the Holy Spirit called Barnabas and Saul to missionary work. It is probable that they were the mediums through whom the Spirit made His desires known.

Paul himself possessed the gift. In **Acts 27: 23** there is recorded one instance in which he was able to predict the shipwreck of the boat on which he was a prisoner-passenger *en route* to Rome, and the astonishing fact, also, that all passengers on board would be saved from drowning. Further references to his prophetic gift are found in **Acts 16: 6, seq.; 18-9; 22: 17.** In these cases, it appears that he obtained the knowledge which informed him of future events by means of visions and dreams. He placed high value on that gift, preferring it to the ability to speak in tongues, another gift he frequently exercised, as we infer from **1 Corinthians 14.**

The Book of Revelation is a product of the spirit of prophecy. It is probably the last produced by one under the influence of the Holy Spirit. If so, Paul's prophecy that "prophecies shall be done away" (**1 Cor. 13: 8**) became history with the writing of that book.

The fact that apostles possessed prophetic gifts was known and accepted by both friends and enemies of the church. Because of the esteem in which inspired men were held, certain "false prophets" appeared on the scene, hoping to profit materially by their counterfeit claims, or to obtain leadership positions by means of which they might subvert the truth as taught by apostles. **1 John 4: 1-3** reveals how deeply the aged apostle was disturbed by them. He warned his readers against their seductive heresies and described the marks by which they might be identified. They denied some of the claims of Jesus to a unique Sonship with God. "Every spirit that confesseth that Jesus Christ is come in the flesh is of God: and every spirit that confesseth not Jesus is not of God: and this is the spirit of the antichrist, whereof ye have heard that it cometh; and now it is in the world already."

This quotation justifies the conclusion that a considerable number who arrogate some prophetic function today, belong in that class of "antichrists." Their finger prints are filed, doubtless in the Unitarian section of heaven's records of theological criminals. Unitarian theology is responsible for at least 90 percent of all the conditions so generally deplored in the Christian world today. It does make a difference what the world thinks about Jesus Christ—whose Son He is. God cares; Christ cares; we also should care.

One other observation on New Testament prophets should be made. While they were Spirit-led in their predictive declarations, they nevertheless remained in personal control of their utterances. **1 Cor. 14: 29-32** asserts that "the spirits of prophets are subject to the prophets." If so, both the content of the message and the timeliness of its delivery must have been governed largely by the good judgment of the prophet. He was more than a mere mouthpiece. A suggestive thought may be found in the bearing of this fact on inspiration.

Our survey of the office and work of both apostles and prophets leads to the judgment that both were temporary, by the very nature of their assignments. The apostles were "witnesses" of the fact that Jesus arose from the dead, thus limiting the number qualified to fill that office to those of that generation.

They were sent forth into areas where churches were to be established, as pioneers in gospel proclamation.

Prophets, on the other hand, appear to have confined their ministries to Christians. They strengthened those suffering persecution, their contact with the eternal world through the Spirit empowering them to bring such assurance to the saints as they needed to enable them to endure. They comforted Christians who suffered martyrdom—the highest honor then open to a Christian.

They may have served also by interpreting the New Dispensation in the light of the Old Covenant, explaining how that "which waxeth aged was nigh unto vanishing away."

It is an interpretive error to try to justify certain ministerial activities in the realm of social, political or economic areas, on the supposition that the examples of some Old Testament prophets who did these things warrant the preacher of the gospel in doing likewise. Old Testament prophets functioned in a theocracy. The government in which they served was both a civil and religious institution. It was as nearly a union of church and state as the world has seen. Moses, as its lawgiver, had legislated for the people, including in his code the ordinances of religion, directions for worship, instruction in morals, civil and humanitarian rules, judicial procedures, sanitary regulations, etc. The Pentateuch, in its single set of commandments and decrees, covered every conceivable need of a people in the state of civilization such as Israel then enjoyed. Under such a governmental set-up, active participation in all matters of social, industrial, political and educational affairs by the prophets, whose

talents always gained for them some special
recognition, was the natural, the logical thing
to expect.

In the church of Christ, the situation is
wholly different. Jesus said His kingdom is
not of this world, thus removing it from political or other this-worldly responsibilities. Let
the politically dead bury their own dead.

Furthermore, the Old Testament prophets
were inspired men. They insisted they were
proclaiming messages received direct from God,
a claim present-day preachers would find some
difficulty in sustaining. They had a "call"
which was special, not general, like that of a
minister of the gospel. Since it is a sort of
favorite indoor sport on the part of some theo-
logians to deny the inspiration of Old Testament seers, explaining it as a mere urge of
conscience, yet exalting their greatness, courage, honesty, influence, etc., it may be well to
note the claims these men made for themselves.
If they were as great as their socially-minded
admirers concede, they must have been truthful
men and at least ordinarily intelligent. Their
assertions of inspiration (the reception of revelations, visions, messages, etc., from God) are
emphatic. They are also astonishingly complete, for no recognized Old Testament seer
has failed to file his credentials when delivering

his prophetic philippics or encouraging by promises of divine help.

Let us begin with Isaiah. He opens his prophecy thus: "The vision of Isaiah, the son of Amoz, which he saw concerning Jerusalem" (**Isa. 1:1**).

In the fourth verse of the first chapter of his book, Jeremiah writes: "The word of the Lord came unto me."

Ezekiel saw "the heavens opened and visions of God," so he affirms in **Ezek. 1:1.**

Daniel's "visions" are too numerous for citation. No author has been more insistent in affirming his contact with God in such a direct way as to obtain wisdom for the guidance of kings, the interpretation of dreams of warning, and the miraculous intervention of the heavenly Father in such protecting care as to spare his life.

Hosea begins his book, "The word of Jehovah that came to Hosea" (**Hos. 1:1**).

Joel declared, "The word of Jehovah that came to Joel," (**Joel 1:1**) made up the contents of his volume.

With trip-hammer force and repetition, Amos affirms that his utterances were inspired: "Thus saith Jehovah," introduces more than a score of his messages. He also asserts that numerous visions came to him. It would be a bold preacher who would make similar claims today.

Obadiah entitles his book, "The Vision of Obadiah," and then proceeds to write, "Thus saith the Lord Jehovah" (**Obad. 1:1**).

In **Jonah 1:1** the statement "The word of Jehovah came to Jonah" is found.

Micah opens his prophecy: "The word of Jehovah that came unto Micah" (**Mic. 1:1**).

Nahum asserts that he received a special revelation: "The book of the vision of Nahum" (**Nah. 1:1**).

Note Habakkuk's statement: "The burden [oracle] which Habakkuk the prophet did see" (**Hab. 1:1**).

Zephaniah writes: "The word of Jehovah that came unto Zephaniah" (**Zeph. 1:1**).

Haggai did not overlook supporting his claim to attention, for he writes: "The word of Jehovah came by Haggai" (**Hag. 1:1**).

Zechariah also heard a message from Jehovah: "Came the word of Jehovah to Zechariah" (**Zech. 1:1**).

And the last of the prophets, Malachi, began his writing thus: "The burden [oracle] of Jehovah came to Malachi" (**Mal. 1:1**).

In the face of the unanimous claims to special revelation, made by every Old Testament prophet, no one who has the slightest

reverence for the Bible can classify these men
with the ministers of today, so far as inspiration and speaking with authority are concerned.
The statement that Old Testament prophets
were not seers is definitely untrue, unless every
one of them made a false claim for himself.
Jesus, on the other hand, accredited them.
"Search the scriptures . . . they testify of me,"
He said to the unbelieving Jews, quoting the
very writings they professed to revere as
inspired, for the very purpose of preparing
that nation to accept Him as Lord. The apostles, preaching to Jews, made regular and consistent appeals to the prophets whom that generation accepted as Spirit-guided men, in support of their thesis that Jesus was the Christ.

Ministers of the Word are called to "preach,"
as were those Old Testament heroes; but they
lack the "vision" those men had. The word
"prophet" was a later name for "seer," as
explained in **1 Sam. 9:9**: "He that is now
called a *prophet* was beforetime called a *seer*.
The "seer" was given a vision of what the
future held in store. His predictive endowment provided him with the necessary credentials to authenticate his message to those he
addressed. It is thus very clear that there were
essential differences between the Old Testament
prophets and the modern preachers.

In **Rom. 12: 6-8** and **1 Cor. 12: 4-11, 28-30,**
the apostle Paul mentions certain "gifts" of the
Spirit—*Charismata*—which seem to have been
imparted either by the laying on of hands
of the apostles, or by direct Spirit enduement.
The exact nature and scope of such gifts are
not clearly defined. They are catalogued as
"wisdom," "knowledge," "faith," "gifts of
healing," "workings of miracles," "prophecy,"
"discerning of spirits," "tongues," "interpreta-
tions of tongues," "helps," "governments."

Some of these gifts could come only by miraculous impartation; others are of such character
that their possession could be available, in a
sense, to all. If these latter were special favors
granted by the Spirit, as the context would
suggest, the miraculous element in them would
be manifested by the *degree* in which they were
possessed rather than in the kind.

This much may be said: that some of them
seem to have been connected with phases of the
ministry of the Word, while others were serv-
iceable more particularly in administering the
affairs of the congregation in the interests of
the membership.

They are always referred to as objective
illustrations of the abundance of divine "grace"
bestowed on those so endued. That it was a
special, therefore temporary, gift is evident

from every passage mentioning it. They were to "pass away."

Next, we pass in our study to those orders or phases of ministering which are permanent. They include those types of service which are as imperative today as they were in the beginning. By their very nature, they are necessary to the continuation of the church. They are found in every congregation of the New Testament era, hence essential to its ministering as a group. The whole church is a ministering agency, but it performs its services through its divinely authorized representatives.

The distinction between temporary phases and permanent orders in ministering is not clearly drawn by the apostle in the quotation at the beginning of this chapter. Both were working together then. It would have been unwise to label apostolic and prophetic ministries as "temporary" in his Epistle. Some ambitious persons would insist that they had already "passed away," and would proceed to improve on the divine order—by creating orders of their own, as was done early in the sub-apostolic age.

Doubtless for that reason, Paul did not raise the question of the permanency of any of the types of ministering. But in his other writings he emphasizes the importance, the honor, and the responsibilities of these phases which are conceded to be permanent.

First of these is that of the "evangelist." As the etymology of the word indicates, evangelists were announcers of "good news" or "good tidings." There is but slight difference in the technical use of "tidings" and "news," but that small distinction as to word content would lead us to prefer "tidings" as a designation for the gospel message. "News" carries the suggestion of freshness, primarily. When first proclaimed, the gospel had that characteristic, of course. But with the passing of time, the message acquired the nature of "tidings," rather than that of "news." Tidings may be very old, but when qualified by the adjective, "good," they are worth receiving. Furthermore, the personal element enters into the meaning of "tidings," suggesting a message or announcement which is carried by a personal representative of the sender. There is an ambassadorial hint in the word. "Good tidings" from God to man should be full of joy.

The joyful content of the gospel is found in the evangelist's proclamation that Jesus of Nazareth had entered the world as both Saviour and Christ. The good tidings of every New Testament evangelist always centered in Jesus as the Christ.

God Himself was an "evangelist" to Abraham (**Gal. 3:8**). A "blessing" to all the world, through his Seed, was pledged to the patriarch, when Jehovah explained His reason for calling Abraham out of Ur.

The promise that his Descendant would bring a blessing to all who desired it would be some compensation for being commanded to leave his kindred, Chaldean culture and a settled life for a hundred years of nomadic uncertainties.

In **Luke 20:1** Jesus is called an "evangelist," as He preached in the temple on Tuesday of that last week of His ministry.

Paul, in **Rom. 1:15,** expresses an earnest desire to "evangelize" in Rome.

Philip, one of the first deacons, was also an "evangelist," laboring in Cæsarea when Paul passed through that city *en route* to Jerusalem (**Acts 21:8**). Earlier, he had evangelized in Samaria and the region from Azotus to Cæsarea, during which evangelistic tour he successfully presented the gospel to the treasurer of Queen Candace of Ethiopia.

Timothy is called an "evangelist" by Paul in **2 Tim. 4:5.**

The work of the evangelist would precede that of the pastor or teacher. Often, he seems to have been an itinerant. Whether his ministry was brief or prolonged in a locality, he was always a recruiting officer for the army of his Lord.

Titus, an evangelist, was authorized by Paul to supervise the organization of churches in the island of Crete. That commission should not be understood as conferring on Titus the administrative authority of a "bishop." There is no evidence that he ever held that office. He was entrusted with the responsibility of "setting in order the things that were wanting in the churches," so that all desirable congregational activities might be carried on, in the absence of apostolic oversight and counsel. He was to "appoint" elders in every city for that purpose. The extent of his participation in the selection of officials would doubtless be the same as that exercised by the apostles in Jerusalem when the first seven deacons were chosen. They "appointed" those whom the congregation had elected, evidently merely approving or ratifying the selection. There is no hint of official meddling, or assertion of authority in the local church. The evangelist would naturally be interested in seeing everything done that would insure the permanence of his evangelistic fruit-age, and to that extent would counsel, advise, perhaps lead, in the proper organization of the church.

Evangelists received their credentials from churches, as in the instance wherein the Antioch church sent Barnabas and Saul out as their representatives; or from the apostles directly, as illustrated by Paul's authorizing Timothy, Titus, Luke, Silas, et al., to do that work. The duties of evangelists are set forth in several Scripture passages, such as **1 Tim. 6: 17-19; 2 Tim. 4: 1, 2; Tit. 1: 13; 2: 15.**

They were to "preach the word, reprove, rebuke, exhort," etc. No phase of kingdom work is more important than that of the evangelist. Consecrated men, with an understanding of the content of the gospel message, and with persuasive ability, whose loyalty to Christ transcends every passion in their souls, are needed today, perhaps more seriously needed than in any previous age. The world needs them. The church must have them. The located minister must evangelize his territory or witness the gradual death of his congregation. That evangelism is one of the permanent phases of ministering needs no proof. In **2 Tim. 2: 2** Paul commissions his son in the gospel to transmit the message entrusted to him to other faithful men who would be able to teach still others also, thus providing for the perpetuation of the work of the evangelist. His work will be needed so long as men sin.

Each generation must hear and heed his message, or be lost. Even if the entire world were genuinely Christian in this generation, the next would need the same gospel message, or it would revert to paganism. There can be no doubt that Christ desires the work to be carried on.

Next in order, as named by Paul, in the passage being studied, come "pastors" and "teachers." These words seem to stand here as synonyms, and will be treated as such. The word "pastor" is tender and heart-warming. It means "shepherd" or "herdsman." By metonymy, it came to be used as a title for the presiding official or leader of a local congregation, because one so honored would have a shepherding concern for the spiritual welfare of the people he served. The Oriental shepherd lived with his sheep night and day. He knew them all by name, and they "knew his voice." The relationship between shepherd and flock has inspired poetic and artistic genius to high levels of achievement.

The welfare of the flock and the profit derived from it depended upon the shepherd. He selected the grazing places and led the sheep to them. At least twice daily, they "passed under his rod" as they answered his roll call. If one were missing, anxious search was begun and ceased not till accounted for. It is not strange that this word became the favorite term used in referring to one who ministered to the Christian flock. Christ found a holy joy in identifying Himself with the humble vocation of the shepherd when He said, "I am the good shepherd." No other word presents Him in His tender relationship to men quite so appealingly. Watchcare, feeding, healing, understanding, companionship, are all wrapped up in it.

Peter, in **1 Pet. 2: 25,** calls Jesus "the shepherd and bishop of our souls." This indicates that, in the mind of Peter, no distinction existed between "shepherd" and "bishop" in an official sense. They referred to the same work in ministering.

The word "bishop" is a functional term. It refers to the work of an individual chosen to exercise supervision, oversight, curatorship or spiritual guardianship over a congregation. Our theological word "episcopal" comes from it. Where the office instead of the one holding it is mentioned, the feminine form of the noun is used, and is translated "bishopric," as in **Acts 1: 20.**

The thought contained in the term seems to be that of a general superintendency. In the church, it applies to spiritual oversight, not

to material, of course.   In **Luke 19:44** and
1 Pet. 2:12 the oversight and inspection of
God over men in their religious lives is described by the writers. The feminine form of
this noun, used in the above passages, is translated "visitation." It adds dignity and responsibility to the office to learn that God Himself
exercises the same function over the church
that men are asked to perform.

Another synonymous word for "bishop" is
one translated "elder" meaning a "senior" or
"older" man. The Greek noun is *presbyteros*
from which we derive our "presbytery," once
used (**1 Tim. 4:14**) in the feminine, referring
to the group of "elders" jointly ruling the congregation. It is evident that spiritual supervision or oversight was entrusted, ordinarily
at least, to men of experience, characterized by
the wisdom which maturity and approved service would instill. That they were the presiding
officers in a church is an accepted historical
fact. No indication that preferential position
or standing was given to one above another,
all constituting a group in which parity among
equals was recognized. It should be noted that
Peter (**1 Pet. 5:1**) calls himself a "fellow-
elder" in writing to those responsible for congregational supervision. He makes no claim
to special administrative or executive authority,

such as we usually associate with the word
"bishop" in these degenerate days. His only
claim to preeminence was that of apostolic
authority *to teach*.

Furthermore, New Testament usage shows
that no distinction in rank was recognized
among "pastors," "bishops," "elders." The
terms were used interchangeably. The pastors
were shepherds of souls. Bishops exercised
oversight or supervision over local congregations of which they were members. The elders
were so designated because of their seniority
in age, wisdom, experience.

Taken together, the three pairs of words:
"pastor-shepherd"; "bishop-overseer"; "pres-
byter-elder"; all denote the official responsibility and service of ministering delegated to
men chosen for that work by the local congregation itself. Any discriminatory place or rank
which may be assigned to those holding such
positions today is entirely without New Testament authority.

When one from among this body of equals
was first exalted above the others, and assumed
the title "the bishop," that evil root of ecclesiasticism which ultimately bore all the poison
fruit of apostasy was planted.

1 Tim. 3: 1-7; Tit. 1: 5-9; 1 Pet. 5: 1-4
summarize the duties of the "pastoral minis-

try." They were to teach, exhort, confute, warn, preach, etc. This phase of ministering was instructional.

This was an administrative trust. In all things, they were to be examples to the flock.

The etymological, functioning and illustrative study of the work of ministering reveals it to be the highest, holiest, most blessed calling of God to man. It entrusts to the minister the introduction of his fellows into covenant relations with God, with their cultural progress, and their guidance in religious activities and true Christian living. There is almost a hint in the Bible that angels envied man this glorious task. The responsibilities of it are sobering. The honor is sufficient. The rewards are abiding. In all the world, there is no area in which men serve that is comparable to that of the Christian ministry.

The located minister, by mutual understanding and arrangement with the congregation, becomes an administrative member of the "pastors" or "elders" of a congregation, exercising the functions or performing the duties they may delegate to him. He acts in their behalf, and under their direction. So long as this simple conception of pastoral work obtains, there can be no danger of an ecclesiasticism maturing.

CHAPTER V

The Message of the Ministry

This chapter is devoted to a study of the *content* of the gospel message which Jesus entrusted to His disciples to be proclaimed after His ascension. The source material for the investigation is the New Testament. It is of vital importance to know exactly *what* Spirit-guided men taught as they went forth in obedience to Jesus' command to fulfill their ministry.

Since the New Testament refers repeatedly to angelic and prophetic announcement of a coming message and Messenger, recorded in the Old Testament, it is consistent and logical to begin with these forecasts. They throw light upon both the message, and the program for its delivery.

The first of these predictions is in **Gen. 3: 15,** where a future penalty on Satan is pronounced. The "Seed" of the woman would, ultimately, "bruise the head of the serpent."

121

Here was a warning, buttressed by the citation of a penalty, against the seduction of a soul to sin. The concern God feels about man's purity of life is revealed in the very beginning. Man was to "subdue and have dominion," but he was expected to execute his trust according to divine instructions, keeping himself pure while so doing.

Gen. 12:3 quotes God as promising Abraham, "In thee and thy seed shall all the families of the earth be blessed." Paul, in **Gal. 3:8**, affirms that in that promise, God "preached the gospel beforehand to Abraham." In verse 16 of the same chapter, he argues that the use of the singular word "Seed" identifies the promised "blessing" with the person of Christ. It was not the Jewish race, not Arab nor Syrian through whom God would bless the families of the earth, but through Christ. It was a very definite and specific reference to a "Descendant" according to the flesh, through whom the "blessing" might be obtained. The content of that pledge was spiritual, for Paul identified it with "justification" or "forgiveness." The passages cited above assure us that the "gospel" would deal with sin and forgiveness.

Isaiah supplies an identifying mark whereby the One through whom the "blessing" should

come might be recognized (**Isa. 7: 14**): "Therefore the Lord himself shall give you a sign:
behold, a virgin shall conceive, and bear a son,
and shall call his name Immanuel." Here is
a positive assertion of a miraculous birth as
arranged for the "son." While it is true that
the word translated "virgin" also means "young
woman," it would be absurdly silly to direct
attention to the fact that a "young woman"
should bear a child as a "sign from God."
"Virgin" gives meaning and point to the
prophecy, and is the only fair translation of
the term.

In **Isa. 9: 6** the prophet returns to his char-
acterization of the unique Personality who was
to be born of a virgin, by outlining the nature
of his official trust. "For unto us a child is
born, unto us a son is given; and the government shall be upon his shoulder: and his name
shall be called Wonderful, Counsellor, Mighty
God, Everlasting Father, Prince of Peace."
Attributes of Deity are ascribed to Him, and
rule in the realm where Deity works is assigned
as His task.

Another prophetic guidepost is found in
Jer. 31: 31-34.

The Hebrew writer (**Heb. 8: 7-13**) quotes
this passage in support of his thesis that
Christ's succession to the seat of authority in

religion was God-approved, "their iniquities will I remember no more." The gospel being "good tidings," the promise of forgiveness of sins in Christ, whereas under the law all had been under condemnation, would indeed meet the requirements of the definition.

Mic. 4: 1, seq., identifies Jerusalem and the temple as the site from which the new covenant should be proclaimed by divine authority. The Pentecost scene is undoubtedly the fulfillment of that prophecy.

In the next chapter (**Mic. 5: 2**) Micàh asserts the eternity of being of Him who was to be born in "Bethlehem Ephrathah," and locates the birthplace of "one come forth unto me that is to be ruler of Israel." These Old Testament citations reveal God's gradual preparation of the world, through prophetic channels, for the coming of His Son. They are germane to the subject matter of this chapter because they constituted a part of the gospel message as found later in the New Testament. No fact is stressed more insistently by New Testament writers than that God had been preparing the nation of Israel for centuries, had it but listened to His teachings, for the coming and mission of Jesus as Christ. We therefore turn now to that first-century testimony.

Luke 1: 31 records an angelic announcement made to Mary that astounded her: "Thou shalt conceive in thy womb, and bring forth a son, and shall call his name JESUS." Knowing her virginity, Mary protested, "How can these things be, seeing I know not a man?" Her own skepticism about the "virgin birth" is understandable. The angel explains that this promised motherhood will be unique, in that her child shall be divinely begotten, and shall bear a name—"The Son of God," indicating the fact.

A similar message was delivered to Joseph by an angel. **Matt. 1: 20, 21:** "That which is conceived in her is of the Holy Spirit. And she shall bring forth a son, and thou shalt call his name JESUS; for it is he that shall save his people from their sins." Once again, the advent of Jesus is heralded as the world's hope for the forgiveness of sin.

Shepherds in Bethlehem pastures were the first to hear the "good news" as a historic fact, instead of a Messianic hope. "There is born to you this day in the city of David a Saviour, who is Christ the Lord" (**Luke 2: 11**). A choir of angels sang their "Glory to God in the highest" anthem immediately following. Thus, to humble men, was announced the glorious news that at last a Saviour, long awaited by pious men, needed since the tragedy of Eden, had come to earth.

When, in due time, He was presented at the temple for legal purification of the mother, and redemption of the Child, Simeon and Anna, aged temple attendants to whom revelation had been made that they should behold their Redeemer before being gathered to their fathers, proclaimed in Him the fulfillment of their hopes.

This study of backgrounds will enable us to appreciate understandingly the unprecedented interest shown by various groups in the birth of this Child.

Thirty years later, John the Baptist appears, bearing witness to both the personality and the mission of Jesus. **John 1: 29:** "John seeth Jesus coming unto him, and saith, Behold the Lamb of God who taketh away the sin of the world."

The Scripture passages studied thus far reveal two tremendously important facts: First, that God, for ages, had been preparing a certain people for this "gospel message." (It may not be out of place to remark that, regardless of the wisdom men may acquire, it is improbable that they shall ever discover a better gospel than that which God worked on for several millenniums.)

Second, that the one theme, running like a holy melody throughout, deals with *sin* and *salvation* from sin through Jesus as Christ.

Any message that forsakes this fundamental theme, therefore, has no right to call itself "the gospel of Christ."

A survey of Jesus' own teaching as to the content of His gospel message is in order here. His epitomized statement of it is found in **Luke 19:10,** where He says, "The Son of man has come to seek and save the lost." Salvaging, therefore, was Jesus' major work. He offered no apology for it; was not ashamed to be found in the company of those who needed saving. To achieve that end, He was willing to die.

If He loved to do one thing, more than another, it was to forgive the sin of a penitent and encourage him to "sin no more." The healing of the Capernaum paralytic and His word to the woman caught in sin make this fact crystal clear. Redemptive work, contemptuously dismissed from the program of some who would "save" the world by education or a change in the social order, occupied His every moment from Jordan to Calvary. He entered a world where blind gropers were being led by blind guides. He declared Himself "the light of the world" and urged men to walk in His illuminated pathway. His Nazareth sermon, recorded in **Luke 4: 16-19,** emphasized His salvaging mission. He told the audience that He had come to "release the captives." Those who heard Him knew that His concern was about men who were captives to sin. The keeper of the Nazareth jail took no steps to frustrate a possible assault on his prison in behalf of its inmates. All who listened to Jesus soon perceived that He was trying to "save" those who were in sin.

It is impossible to emphasize this fact over-much.

The "Great Commission," some form of which has been preserved in every Gospel, sent the disciples forth on a salvaging work. "He that believeth and is baptized shall be saved," indicates salvation as an end. They were to labor to that purpose.

He had already instructed them in the technique of making disciples, the plan He had adopted for world salvation.

The minister of today should repeat often the closing words of the Great Commission: "Lo, I am with you alway, even to the end of the world." They are both comforting and sobering. The assurance of His personal presence, even though unseen, would comfort and sustain those to whom He spoke. Every one of His post-resurrection appearances was a visible demonstration that He was remembering it. He would become visible to them when they were not expecting Him, and disappear without seeming to go away. They would be sobered by it also, for it was as if He had said, "I shall be watching you constantly, checking up on your faithfulness and loyalty." Those who minister in this day should find that same comfort and admonition which those first disciples experienced in recalling His promise.

Jesus' concern that His message should be transmitted correctly is shown by the caution He took to prevent imperfect proclamation of it. It was to be broadcast fully, but not prematurely.

In **Acts 1: 4, 5,** it is recorded, "He charged them not to depart from Jerusalem, but to wait for the promise of the Father, which, said he, ye heard from me: for John indeed baptized with water; but ye shall be baptized with the Holy Spirit not many days hence."

This restraining order was given, lest in their eagerness to tell of His resurrection, they should either arouse false hopes among the people, or misinterpret its spiritual significance. The "promise of the Father" referred to may be found in **John 14: 16, 26; 16: 7-13.** As they went forth to "witness" for Christ, the apostles would need the personal, controlling influence of the Holy Spirit to guide them, to refresh their memories, to aid in the understanding of gospel truth, and to enable them to speak the right word when under trial, or preaching in open, free assemblies.

Their enduement with "power from on high" on the day of Pentecost lifted the barrier behind which they had been waiting impatiently for the word to "go." There can be no shadow of doubt that the words spoken on that occasion by the apostles, preaching under the spell of Spirit control, were the infallible proclamation of the "gospel message" which Jesus had authorized them to deliver.

All their subsequent preaching, as recorded in Acts and the Epistles, was entirely consistent with that Pentecostal sermon.

They preached "the gospel," and nothing else. It is neither bigotry nor intolerance to affirm that ministers today have no divine authority for preaching anything other than a New Testament message.

Jesus' promise of Holy Spirit guidance to His disciples, and the Pentecostal fulfillment of His pledge, are sufficient to attest the inspiration of the men who have left us the New Testament, and accredit their writings as having divine authority.

Anything more, or less, than the "gospel" which those men preached can not be "the gospel of Christ." Paul emphatically denounced either man or angel who should preach any other gospel as meriting the curse of God. *It does make a difference what we preach.*

We are now ready to "search the scriptures" to learn what the gospel of Jesus and Paul and other disciples was. That discovered, we shall know exactly what the message of the ministry today should be, for the "faith" we declare was "once for all delivered," indicating finality for it, both as to content and form. When God delivers anything "once for all" it is perfect, incapable of improvement or revision.

It was a "committed" gospel. In **1 Tim. 1:11,** Paul refers to "the gospel of the blessed God, which was *committed to my trust.*" Later, in verse 18 of the same chapter, he enjoins, "This charge I *commit unto thee, my child, Timothy.*" Similar instruction is given in **2 Tim. 2:2.** "The things which thou hast heard from me, among many witnesses, *the same commit thou to faithful men,* who shall be able to teach others also." No greater precaution than that which Paul exercised, to guarantee the continuing proclamation of the gospel which he had received, can be imagined.

He personally selected and trained those who must carry on after his death. They were cautioned to be careful in the selection and teaching of the men who were to become the custodians of this carefully guarded message after their departure. Both Jesus and Paul demanded of the ministry the proclamation of the gospel unchanged.

This conclusion is undeniable: the true gospel message was not something that men could *discover,* not the *product of human wisdom,* but something God had revealed in the person of His Son Jesus. In our search to discover what this "committed gospel" was, and is, we must begin with the message delivered on Pentecost. There is no other place where it is recorded so fully. The entire message can not be found in the Gospels, for Jesus pledged the apostles to send His Spirit to guide them into all truth, that they might interpret and apply His principles to those who were to be saved by them. Not that any contradictions or inconsistencies exist between the teaching of Jesus and His disciples. But the message He desired to have proclaimed after His ascension must be found, if anywhere, in the teaching of His apostles.

The heart of the Pentecostal preaching was the absolute Lordship of Jesus. Peter's sermon climaxed, "Let all the house of Israel, therefore, know assuredly, that God hath made him both Lord and Christ, this Jesus whom ye crucified" (**Acts 2: 36**). The word "Lord" identified Him with Deity. "Christ" identified Him with the Jewish "Messiah," of whom the prophets had written. Both sermon and scene proved the claim to be true. Around that fact, all genuine preaching since that day has centered. The hearing multitude believed, and were "pricked in their hearts."

The conviction of sin (a part of the office work of the Holy Spirit, **John 16: 8**) led to their anguished cry for directions as to what they should do. The inspired answer was plain and unequivocal: "Repent ye, and be baptized, every one of you, in the name of Jesus Christ, unto the remission of your sins, and ye shall receive the gift of the Holy Spirit. For the promise is to you, and to your children, and to all that are afar off, even as many as the Lord our God shall call unto him" (**Acts 2: 38, 39**). The "gospel" was to "proclaim release to the captives" of sin; to give new hope to the broken-hearted who were despairing of forgiveness. Primarily, it had to do with man's relationship to God, for until that was made right, none of His relationships to man would be right.

Following the healing of the lame man at the temple gate a few days later, Peter exhorted his hearers, "Repent ye, therefore, and turn again, that your sins may be blotted out, that so there may come seasons of refreshing from the presence of the Lord; and that he may send the Christ who hath been appointed for you, even Jesus: whom the heavens must receive until the times of restoration of all things" (**Acts 3:19**). Again, the forgiveness of sins is central in the preaching.

Another incidental allusion to the apostolic preaching is found in **Acts 4:1, 2**: "The priests and the captain of the temple and the Sadducees came upon them, being sore troubled because they taught the people, and proclaimed in Jesus the resurrection of the dead."

It was a *Jesus-centered message* that caused the opposition. None of the persecutors would have objected, seriously, to an abstract doctrine affirming a resurrection; nor to a speculative discourse on "immortality." But they refused to permit the name of Jesus to be coupled with the resurrection teaching, in any causal relationship.

That, however, was the core of the message—a divine Personality, offering forgiveness and promising eternal life.

In **1 Cor. 2:1, 2**, Paul retold the Corinthians, "I was determined to know nothing among you but Jesus Christ, and him crucified."

It was not a dead Christ whom Paul preached, but a living One, ascended, ruling, to return when "all things were in subjection."

Stephen's defense, as recorded in **Acts 7,** was a historical indictment of Israel for having rejected both the prophets and Christ.

Like Peter's Pentecost sermon, it "pricked them to the heart," but with very different results. The sin of the Jews, responsibility for which they have disclaimed through the centuries, was the rejection of Jesus as their Messiah or Christ. Inspired ministers appear to have looked upon such sin as unforgivable. If it was unpardonable then, it can be no mere "fault" or "matter of indifference so long as the heart is right" in this day.

In **Acts 8** Luke has left a record of Philip's preaching to the eunuch. But all he says of the sermon is that "he began at the same scripture [**Isa. 53: 7, seq.**] and preached unto him Jesus." The incident starts with "preaching Jesus" and closes with the baptism of the eunuch into Christ. Christ only, again. In the sermon, however, he must have preached Jesus as the One with authority to forgive sins, demanding obedience as conditional thereto. The desire of the eunuch to be baptized indicates that Philip's sermon was the same as that of Peter on Pentecost. Nothing is clearer than

that Philip's preaching was for the purpose of
persuading the eunuch to accept Jesus as
Messiah and Lord.

In commissioning Paul (**Acts 26:18**) Jesus
said, "I am sending thee unto the Gentiles, to
open their eyes and turn them from darkness
unto light and from the power of Satan unto
God, that they may obtain remission of sins
and an inheritance among them that are sancti-
fied by faith in me."

In **1 Cor. 15:1, seq.**, Paul restates his "gospel," which he insists he had declared unto
them when in their midst.   What was it?
"I delivered unto you first of all that which
also I received: that Christ died for our sins
according to the scriptures; and that he was
buried; and that he hath been raised on the
third day according to the scriptures; and that
he appeared," etc.   He who asserted that "in
nothing was I behind the chiefest of the apostles," began and continued his ministry with
exact knowledge of the content of his gospel;
and it was limited to Christ, crucified, buried,
risen, ascended, that the fountain of forgiveness might be opened.   His "gospel" was the
"good tidings" that a way of escape from the
guilt and bondage of sin had at last been
revealed from heaven, in the person of Jesus
Christ.   The "evangel" of every New Testa-

ment minister was "evangelistic." Without exception, they proclaimed the terms of forgiveness as being faith in Jesus as the Christ, the uniquely divine Son of God; repentance from sin; confession of faith in Christ; baptism into Christ. These were Jesus' own terms, specified in His amnesty proclamation to sinners, signed with the ink of His own blood, and recorded in heaven. Those marks of identification of His "heirs" are written in the will which He personally probated in the court of God. Ministers of today should not (and conscientious ones will not) yield to any demand to alter that will. No one on earth has authority to add a codicil to that will. Therefore, in receiving penitents into the church Jesus established, in a local congregation of which he may be minister, the loyal preacher will neither lower nor raise the standard Jesus Himself erected.

We now come to the cultural phases of New Testament ministering. Its subject matter is summarized by Jesus in the comprehensive phrase, "All things whatsoever I have commanded you," referring to what they were to "teach" those who were baptized.

As we have observed, Jesus' agenda for His ministers had two assignments: First, to "teach" as evangelists, persuading men to

accept the forgiveness of sin by obedience to
the gospel; second, to "teach" His commandments and ideals having to do with "the perfecting of the saints unto the work of ministering, to the building up of the body of Christ;
till all attain unto the unity of faith, unto a
fullgrown man, unto the fulness of Christ,"
that all the body may be fitly joined together
in building itself up in love.

Newborn babes were to be fed "the sincere
milk of the word." This diet for infant
Christians should be administered with the
"gentleness of a nurse caring for her own
children," and consist of counsel upon the sim-
plest matters of Christian conduct. **1 Corinthians** is perhaps the best sample of such
"milk" for spiritual babes. The membership
of that church had just recently been lifted out
of pagan religious thought and life. The high
idealism of Christianity was new to them.
They had scarcely learned to walk in a strait
way. They needed to be taught the sin of
factionalism, spiritual pride, personal purity in
morals, indulgence in drink, idolatry, resort to
civil courts, divorce, the perils attending indis-
criminate eating of meat which had been first
offered to idols, brazen defiance of social customs on the part of the women, turning the
Lord's Supper into an orgy, misuse of "spiritual

gifts," Christian liberality, etc. Almost all the things here condemned had been considered moral or permissible by the pagan faiths formerly held.

More mature members of the body of Christ were to be instructed in the practical doctrines and hopes of the gospel. **Tit. 2: 11-15** may be cited as an example of this sort of teaching. "For the grace of God hath appeared, bringing salvation to all men, instructing us, to the intent that, denying ungodliness and worldly lusts, we should live soberly and righteously and Godly in this present world; looking for the blessed hope and appearing of the glory of the great God and our Saviour, Jesus Christ; who gave himself for us, that he might redeem us from all iniquity, and purify unto himself a people for his own possession, zealous of good works. But these things speak and exhort and reprove with all authority."

Christians were to live "in the Spirit," whose fruits are catalogued in **Gal. 5: 22** as consisting in "love, joy, peace, longsuffering, kindness, goodness, faithfulness, meekness, self-control."

The cardinal virtues of honesty, industry, thrift, sobriety, chastity, generosity, etc., were urged on the new Christians and old alike, as distinguishing marks between them and the

practices of the pagan world, out of which
they had come.

Romans 12 is an exalted example of Christian indoctrination on the weighty matters of
the Christian life.

The teaching of Jesus and the apostles on
the relationships between Christians, and
between them and non-Christians in industrial
affairs, merits study and analysis.

The first thing noticed is that they always
emphasized *obligations* more than *rights*. They
esteemed it better to suffer for well-doing than
for evildoing. A mile more than courtesy
prescribed was to be traveled as an expression
of good will. A robe, in addition to the coat
adjudged as due the plaintiff, was to be presented by the defendant, as a courteous apology
for the wrong done, according to court decree.
Debt was advised against. Laboring to earn
something to give to him that had need, was
made a basic principle for both the acquisition
and distribution of property. Slaves were
advised to work in the interest of their masters,
"not with eye service, as men pleasers," but
because they owed that sort of loyalty.

Masters were admonished to be just, even
generous, to their slaves.

Of course, the slavery in which the Christian of the first century found himself involved was a wholly different set-up from that which once existed in this country. There was no racial, often no social distinction between master and slave. Such a thing as having been born into slavery, or being racially subject to it, does not seem to have entered into apostolic treatment of the subject.

There appears to be an assumption that the relation of slave to master rested on some moral obligation, perhaps either in the discharge of a debt, or a voluntary exchange of labor for a specified wage. The point we are making is that in apostolic teaching, more emphasis was given to obligations than to rights—an emphasis that assuredly makes for peace, not for strife. Perhaps a clue for the minister today may be found in that fact. If he majors on teaching the duties of oppressors rather than on exciting the oppressed, he is more likely to be one of the blessed "peace-makers," in whose company he may justifiably seek a fellowship.

Nothing in the New Testament justifies the belief that either Jesus or the apostles ever showed any class partisanship or preferences. They esteemed men in every group as being under the same law to God and by Him held to accountability for the faithful discharge of every duty imposed on them by their position.

It may seem strange to some who have yielded to the pressure to become partisans for certain groups in economic or social life, that no New Testament writers alluded to the agitation in labor circles in their day, notwithstanding they were much the same as we are experiencing now. We know of at least eighty-seven labor unions operating in Rome when Paul was there as a prisoner, among them a tent-makers' union!

Strikes and lockouts were of frequent occurrence. Minimum wage laws were being made, maximum selling prices decreed, production and importation limits were specified; in short, the first century had labor and capital differences almost identical with ours. The absolute silence of Christ and His apostles on these conditions is astonishing. We know their sympathies were always with the poor, the oppressed, the unfortunate, the sick, the underprivileged, the dispossessed. Their refusal to become partisans in industrial and social conflicts can not be explained on the ground of indifference to the injustices being suffered.

In dealing with that crisis, as with every other serious situation, they took the long view. They always located the cause of every social disease, and prescribed a radical cure, not interesting themselves in palliatives or anodynes. They knew that the only solution for every problem of capital and labor, as well as that arising out of social injustice, would be found only in the regeneration of those involved, and the adoption of a code of unselfishness.

An illustration of the practical working out of their ideals may be found in the case of the communism tried out in the Jerusalem church where certain widows were being neglected. It grew out of Jesus' teaching that "It is more blessed to give than to receive."

It is significant that those who entered into that compact were those who *had,* not those who had not. It did not arise out of a demand made by the poor on the rich. It seems to have been a voluntary association formed to assist their own needy. As such, it was as far removed from the program advocated by today's communists as unselfishness is removed from selfishness. It appears to have been a temporary expedient, not wholly different from the "community chest" plan used in some cities. No reference to anything similar to it is found elsewhere in New Testament literature. It can not be cited, with fairness, as an example of an ideal Christian order.

It evidently failed, if intended to be permanent. If temporary, to meet a tragic emergency, it was a success. But the wise minister will be cautious about using it as either an argument for or illustration of what passes as communism today.

In these perilous days of revolutionary proposals and experiments, the minister should withhold partisan support from special industrial and legislative programs championed by any class or group. Not to exercise "discretion"; but to apply himself to the more fundamental task of regenerating all classes. He can do no better than to follow the example of Jesus Himself, who positively refused to see men in classes or strata. Each individual was viewed as a personality responsible to God and man for right conduct.

To Jesus, every man was a creature made in God's image, capable of redemption, even though a sinner; and once regenerated, he would act as a son of God.

Jesus did not prescribe *social remedies for social ills*. He knew that social injustice would not be removed by the substitution of one social order for another. Of what use would such a remedy be, when the administration or application of it must be left to the same individuals or groups who are responsible for the state of injustice complained of? By no stretch of the imagination can we conceive of Jesus

petitioning Cæsar to revise the taxing laws
as a means of abolishing graft as practiced by
the publicans. His plan was to invite Himself
to a meal with the grafter, convert him, and
show him what honest administration of the
law meant. Jesus' entire energy was spent in
changing men, knowing that desirable changes
in laws and procedures would follow as surely
as effect follows cause. According to Jesus,
in both His teaching and example, society can
be regenerated only by regenerating its individual units, not by legislation or retaliatory
measures.

It may not be impertinent to raise the
question whether ministers and reformers in
general have not erred in depending too much
on statute or constitutional alteration, as a
means for the abolition or control of crime and
immorality.

Is it not possible that the cause of sobriety
would be further advanced today if the church
had taught the immorality of the beverage use
of alcohol as industriously as she did the abolition of the saloon? If the minister leads and
persuades the congregation he serves to total
abstinence, leaving Cæsar to enforce his own
legal enactments for narcotic control, is he
following more nearly the example of Jesus and
His apostles than he would be by leading in

law enforcement campaigns? At least, the matter is worthy of prayerful thought.

There is a temptation to the ministry of today, especially to the young men who have been taught to see the injustice suffered by the economically disinherited, the underprivileged and the socially discriminated against, to take up the trade of "society tinkering" instead of following the vocation to which they have been called—proclaimers of a divine evangel. In many influential places, emphasis is on reform instead of regeneration. The preacher's commission deals with the latter. The reformer is vocal in his advocacy of "the kingdom of God," which he would introduce by a "social gospel" program. That there is a social message and objective in the gospel is not in dispute. One phase of the gospel has to do with conduct, and all conduct is social. It is heartening to note the awakening of conscience on the part of people in seats of authority and leadership to the social inequalities existent. Efforts to ameliorate these conditions should receive encouragement from all good people.

But there is a subtle fallacy in the reasoning of some, of which ministers should beware. It is the assumption that when social conditions are made ideal, the kingdom of God will be here, and that its coming depends upon the introduction of ideal social relations. A recent writer says: "Give men a guarantee of security and the incentive to greed and covetousness will be removed, and the evil will vanish with the incentive." He failed to see the fact that a man "socially secure" might still covet his neighbor's wife, and that his possession of "security" might contribute to his obtaining what he coveted. Much inexcusable blame may be attached to society, but its share in and responsibility for sin may be exaggerated easily. The preacher should never forget that Satan is still the adversary of man, and is responsible for sin. The temptation of Jesus, so terrific that hunger fled Him for forty days, did not arise out of His social or material environment, yet His material station was not above that of those who charge all their derelictions to society. Men sin when their hearts are impure. The gospel works in hearts, to purify them. Men are saved or lost, because of the state of their hearts. In Jesus' picture of Paradise, He brought into the closest possible relations in the eternal world two whose material possessions and social standing were at opposite extremes in this world. Abraham was rich and a companion of kings. Lazarus was poor and a social outcast. Yet it seems that neither the privileges of the one nor the privations of the other prevented them from being justified by the same faith.

This is no time to encourage the dissipated, the disgruntled, the shiftless, the envious, to attach all blame for their condition on the church and society. Jesus commands all men, everywhere, regardless of environment, to repent and obey the gospel. They have the will to do so, *if they will.* The minister will not serve those whose interests he has at heart by pulpit fulminations against an order which needs readjustment. He should imitate the example of Jesus when the man came to Him asking for intervention in the settling of an estate. He flatly refused, but gave counsel about the dangers of covetousness. "What is that to thee, follow thou me" is another echo of Jesus' refusal to be drawn away from His purpose of calling all men to discipleship. That came first. It is not reorganization that society needs; it is regeneration. The Christ whom the minister should proclaim to every one, rich and poor, high and low, cultured and ignorant alike, is able and anxious to regenerate it. But he does not do it *en masse*—just one person at a time. If the minister fails to drive this truth home to his hearers, no one else will. The salvation of all depends upon his faithful and persistent iteration of Jesus' plan.

Let us look a little closer at the New Testament teaching on the subject of "the kingdom of God."

A "kingdom" postulates a king. The "kingdom of God" postulates a kingdom in which God rules. In the "kingdom of God and of Christ" there is joint rule of two, working together, ruling as one. A "kingdom" must also have citizens or subjects. Jesus came to establish God's kingdom on earth. So declared John the Baptist, Jesus Himself, and the apostles. What was Jesus' agenda? He began by calling men to become disciples. He claimed divine authority to make this demand, and proved it by His miracles, God also thus approving His kingly rights.

Jesus' demand that any man who would become His disciple must deny himself (and that includes the whole personality), take up a cross and follow Him; His stern statement to a man of fine character and culture that even he (Nicodemus) must be born again; that no branch can bear fruit except it abide in him; that he who hath not the Son hath not life; that no one cometh to the Father save through the Son; these and a multitude of similar affirmations warrant the conclusion that discipleship is absolutely essential to citizenship in Christ's kingdom.

There is a basic truth which many "kingdom" strategists have covered up in the rubbish of the social temple they are striving to build, viz., that no one will ever really act as a Christian until he becomes one. That one's life is definitely tied up to his faith, and that "without faith it is impossible to please God."

It is impossible to overemphasize this truth: that *no one can be in the kingdom of God who is not in Jesus Christ*. Citizenship privileges belong to citizens only, whether it be in an earthly or in a heavenly kingdom. All who would become citizens of Christ's kingdom must enter at the port of discipleship, forswear all allegiance to any other king, and take the oath of allegiance to Christ as the One having "all authority in heaven and on earth." It is high time preachers stop trying to smuggle into His kingdom men who reject the divine authority of Christ.

Christ's kingdom comes only to those in whose hearts and programs He enters and rules, without rivals.

A corollary, hinted at, but not definitely stated, growing out of this study is this: that *in all His teachings, Jesus never legislated for any but His disciples*. He issued a call to all men to discipleship. If they refused to hear it, He had no further word for them. It is a waste of time to look for grapes on thorns, or figs on thistles. The lamentable failure of every attempt to remedy social, industrial, political, racial or religious evils by compromise, concession, conference, treaty, conformity or rebellion is a commentary on the futility of human wisdom to deal with evil, written in more than nineteen hundred annual volumes. "The world by wisdom knew not God," nor can it lift itself out of the almost maddeningly chaotic conditions now obtaining by its own resourcefulness. Wars have failed of their ends. Treaties have been scrapped as unenforceable. Gentlemen's agreements among diplomats have not been respected. Compromises between conflicting interests have been unsatisfactory to all concerned, and have been accepted no longer than necessary to find some excuse for a new approach.

The making of new world maps, with artificial national boundary lines, have not prevented revolution. In the face of these facts, it should not be difficult to understand why Jesus and His inspired teachers seemed to have little concern about forms of government, legislation, or the social order. They knew that no state, in its laws and administrative programs, could ever be better than the moral qualities of the men who are responsible for

them. They offered both majors and minors
in regenerative effort in their seminars in
human conduct.

If any one ever understood what Jesus meant
by the "kingdom of God," it was His disciples.
As loyal followers, they would begin to execute
His orders immediately upon their enduement
by the Holy Spirit. What did they do? They
began with evangelization. Their next emphasis was on "culturing" the evangelized in Christian graces and virtues. They, at least, believed
they were obeying the will of Christ and were
guided therein by the Holy Spirit. Christ's
kingdom was to be composed of a group of
spiritually-minded disciples, operating within all
other group life, whatever the basis of its
organization.

A citizen of the kingdom of God had a dual
responsibility: First, a spiritual obligation to
its King and his fellow subjects; second, social,
economic, political, et al. obligations to the
secular group of which, by virtue of residence,
occupation, or other status, he might be a part.
No obligation to Christ would interfere with
his obligation to human group life. But beware
of trying to reverse that statement.

The first ministers ceased to stress "kingdom" after Pentecost and devoted themselves
to building the church. They were a unit in

believing that the way to establish the kingdom was by evangelizing folk and organizing them into local congregations. If their procedure was right, the minister has little difficulty in deciding what Christ expects of him today, for the gospel has not been changed in content or method of extension.

As ministers, we have Christ's own remedy for the correction of every evil among men, directly under our eyes, whenever we read our New Testaments. Our commission from on high is to go into all the world and make disciples of every creature. Our task is divinely simple and divinely comprehensive.

When we are actually converting souls to Christ, we are doing more for world peace, more toward the settlement of labor troubles, more to bring about ideal social conditions than all other agencies combined. Our message is one of individual, personal salvation. When that is properly done, there will be no serious conflicts among men. Conflicts will not cease till that is done. We have a monopoly on the message men should have. They may not receive it, but that is no fault of ours, if we offer it to them with devout abandon. We have been assigned a great work to do, and should waste no time in fruitless and delaying conferences on the plains of modern Onos.

The "social gospel" can not establish the kingdom of God, for the simple reason that Christ did not come to establish an earthly order of government or control. He explained, "The kingdom of God is within you." Then it is not an outward or human control of conduct and human relationships.

The kingdom of God is that state of life wherein the will of Jesus Christ is made the basis of all conduct. It will come just as rapidly, and only to the extent that men accept Christ as Lord and Saviour. This is the minister's social message for today.

CHAPTER VI

Who Should Preach?

In this chapter, the theme of ministering is narrowed down to those specialized phases of service in which full time is devoted to the church, such as that of pastors, evangelists, or others engaged in organizational activities which are designed to assist or supplement the work of ministers and churches.

Here, as heretofore, we turn to New Testament teaching and example for our source material. All ministering that is acceptable to Christ must have the seal of His own authority upon it, and the Gospels and Epistles contain all the information that is available which bears upon what He approved.

We ask these records who should preach. What qualifications ought a herald of the cross of Christ to possess? By what standards may a young man who aspires to the highest of callings judge himself in making final decision as to fitness for the work? What character-

istics or endowments should he exhibit to justify his friends and the officials of the local
church of which he is a member in encouraging
his purpose to preach?

The importance of prayerful stock-taking
of everything that enters into his personality
can not be overemphasized.

The number of men in the ministry who,
for one reason or another, are misfits, is unfortunate, often tragic.

It is a serious offense against the young
man himself to encourage him to preach, if by
nature, training, or traits of character that
will render his services undesirable, he is
unfitted for evangelistic or pastoral responsibilities. It is better, more honorable, to dis-
courage him, and thus possibly prevent a good
youth from becoming a pessimistic critic of
the church, going through life as a pitiable
misfit.

Let us begin at the beginning. First of all,
he must have *denied himself*. Those words
mean exactly what they say. Only superficially
do they apply to what is often termed "self-
denial," in which certain amusements, indulgences, ambitions, habits, etc., are involved
The ascetic abstainer is not the type approved
by Christ. Such a one may be indulging "self"
by his very austerity. He is misled by his

negative attitudes, believing them to be an expression of holiness. The Pharisee who prayed to be seen of men probably denied himself many things, but was damned by his pride. There is no more subtle or deceptive form of pride than that which parades before the people masked as "humility." Heaven is not won so much by things undone or refused, as by things done. The closing paragraphs of the twenty-fifth chapter of Matthew make this crystal clear.

To "deny one's self" means that all selfishness must be cast out. Of course, it will include the banishment of sinful indulgences, of vice in all its forms, of everything that is harmful to one's self or to others. But it means vastly more than that. Ambition must be slain and aspiration enthroned in its place. Nothing can be done that is motivated by self-interest.

We can do no better here than to study the subject in the concrete, as presented in the case of Saul of Tarsus.

Something happened to him that memorable day as he was approaching Damascus and was overpowered by a miraculous light from heaven. Though blinded by that light, he saw with other than physical eyes an unknown Person who challenged him by saying, "Saul, Saul, why persecutest thou me?"

When asked by Saul to identify Himself, He replied, "I am Jesus, whom thou persecutest."

What a surprise that was to the devout Pharisee! In the Old Testament it is written, "No man can look upon the face of God and live." To "see the face of God" was equivalent to a death notice, as understood by men like Manoah, who feared a speedy death for himself and wife because an angel had appeared to them with an announcement from Jehovah. But Paul's autobiographical note in **Gal. 2: 20,** in which he writes "it is no longer I that live, but Christ liveth in me," hints at a different interpretation of the Old Testament statement. When he saw God, in the person of His Son, Paul no longer wanted to live. He preferred to let Him who had appeared live in him instead. In that moment, Paul voluntarily died, and Christ thenceforth lived in him instead of "self."

So must "self" die in every worthy minister of Christ. The clearer his own vision of Christ, the less he desires to live for anything or any person but Christ. His continuing prayer is that Christ may achieve through him, a surrendered, but volunteer, slave counting not his own life dear to himself if by his service Jesus may be exalted as Christ. How it rejoices his heart to see those with and for whom he is ministering, obedient from their own hearts, and thus honoring his Master, Christ!

Thereafter, as Paul affirmed later, he counted all things but refuse that he "might gain Christ and be found in him."

Such annihilation of self as is found in Paul is the concrete object lesson illustrative of the meaning of "self-denial."

In fact, this is the basic demand Jesus has made of every one. "If any man will come after me, let him deny himself, and take up his cross daily, and follow me." That was the tuition payment He required of all who sought to be enrolled in His school of "disciples." It was a dual process of emptying and filling. When self departed, Christ entered. Then the disciple took up his own cross. The cross was an instrument upon which a man might die. If the disciple carried that cross everywhere he went, he would always have that instrument of self-destruction at hand if the old "self" showed signs of reviving.

Just what did Jesus mean by "taking up" a personal "cross"? To Jesus, the *cross was His mission.* He came to earth, in human form, that He might go to Calvary. That was His earthly destination. It was on the cross, as He was about to "yield up His spirit," that He said, "It is finished." His supreme purpose

in coming to man had been accomplished. A
finished program, a finished mission, a finished
life. It was His *mission* that led Him to that
central cross on Calvary. In the accomplishment of that mission, He died.

From that, it may be deduced that the
"cross" which every disciple must "take up,"
is the special, personal mission God had in
mind for him when he entered upon life. The
disciple's "cross" is the *disciple's "mission."*
the *minister's "cross"* is the *minister's "mission."* In taking up that cross, the minister
pledges his Lord that he will go wherever he
is ordered or providentially led to go; that he
will do whatever he is sure his Lord will
approve; that he will teach, preach, only that
which is authorized in the Word he is entrusted
to proclaim. By doing that "daily," self will
remain entombed and Christ will be "living"
in him.

We must not overlook the fact that Jesus
denied Himself, for there seem to have been
times when He was struggling for self-mastery.
In the garden of Gethsemane He prayed that
a certain cup pass without His partaking. Was
"self" stirring? Was it a moment of terrible
temptation? If we imagine that merely because
He was the Son of God His human temptations were less than ours, we err. If "He

was tempted in all points as we," the trial must have been as great in both kind and degree. He had said in declaring His mission, "I came not to do mine own will but the will of him who sent me." This selflessness came to His rescue in that hour of Gethsemane need, for immediately after petitioning the cup to pass, He amended His prayer saying, "Nevertheless, not as *I will,* but as *thou wilt.*" From that moment He seems to have been ready for the cross, and a few hours later finds Him upon it, atoning for the sin of the world, fulfilling His mission of "seeking and saving the lost." Likewise, a true minister of his gospel is never more Christlike than when he is fulfilling his ministerial mission in seeking and saving the lost.

Let us now take a look at those whom Jesus chose to be His apostles, and at the men they selected to be their helpers and successors. The first thing we observe is that they were *all men.* Not one woman was invited to serve in the capacity of public ministering as an apostle or preacher of the Word. That can not be explained as an oversight, nor as a diplomatic concession to the social customs of the age. Jesus was no opportunist. He did, however, honor women. He encouraged them to do what every ideal woman finds her supreme joy in doing—"ministering of her substance."

Woman's "substance" may consist of her property, her counsel, her companionship, her inspiring presence, her comforting power, her sharing in privation or suffering, her intuitive perception of human qualities in men, her trusting worship, her devotion to those she loves, her joy in self-effacement. The ideal woman is happiest in being a "helpmeet," the very thing for which she was created. Real success, true happiness, the most fruitful service, can not be realized by perverting any divine order or plan. Those immortal women of the New Testament who "followed him" found the reward sought in the exalted privilege of looking after His needs, rather than in official or administrative activity. Did they see that He ate, when He forgot to be hungry in His absorption in His task? Did they provide a clean robe to replace one soiled by travel? Did they prepare a restful rug of refreshing softness for His bed? Were they concerned about His health? How many, and not unprofitable questions arise when we try to visualize their "ministering." An ambitious woman who merges herself into such services as indicated above may be comforted by the assurance that in so doing she comes nearer being "great," as Jesus defined it, than she could be in any public station. The Master gratefully and graciously accepted the service of those Godly women who were attracted to Him, but in choosing administrative officers, or calling volunteers for the exacting duties and demands of public ministration in preaching, evangelizing, "ruling" in churches, He selected men, in every instance. Not because of a scarcity of women followers, but because the responsibilities of such directing and administrative positions can be discharged better by men. Perhaps less religious confusion would exist today if natural differences between the sexes had been respected in the division of Christian responsibilities.

The incident in which Jesus addressed a rebuking word to His mother at Cana is apropos here. When she volunteered a hint that He might relieve an embarrassed groom whose supply of wine had run out, thus venturing to direct His activity, He replied "Woman, what have I to do with thee?" Woman-like, she was concerned that the social hour be a success. Jesus' thought was upon His work, and He was waiting the proper time to drop a miraculous suggestion as to His personality. Notwithstanding certain exceptions that may be cited, administrative ability and executive success are associated with masculinity. They are not admirable feminine traits.

At the risk of joining the company of those who rush in where angels fear to tread, judgment is here expressed that if all administrative and directing authority in the churches through the centuries had been left where Jesus and the apostles assigned it, the will of Christ would have been followed more nearly. It is true that in Christ there is no male nor female, so far as the blessings and promises of the gospel are concerned. But entrance into Christ does not *change* sex, nor alter fundamental sexual characteristics. What is here affirmed is that it is a perilous adventure to depart from Christ's program for each sex in His church.

The men whom Jesus called for public ministration were drawn from different vocational and class levels. Some were fishermen; others from village and rural life; one was from official rank; one was a natural thief; the greatest of them all was the product of a noted school, quite possibly a Sanhedrist. These were enrolled in His school for training, and all had the same doctrinal and cultural curriculum assignments.

Our attention next centers on the qualifications of those ministers chosen by divine direction.

First of all, they had a genuine faith in the deity of Jesus. His absolute authority as Lord and Master was never questioned. "We believe, therefore do we speak" was their apology. "I know whom I have believed" was Paul's defense. "Let all the house of Israel therefore know assuredly, that God hath made him both Lord and Christ, this Jesus, whom ye crucified," was the bold declaration of unstable Simon, who became Peter. Later, he gave negative affirmation to the same faith, and banished all religious competitors of his Lord by exclaiming: "There is none other name under heaven, that is given among men, wherein we must be saved." Matthew asserted that Jesus had "authority both in heaven and on earth," in quoting Christ's own words. The mystic John, with reverent conviction, wrote "The Word became flesh and dwelt among us." Every man who ministered in the New Testament church accepted the word of Christ as truth, absolute, authoritative, final, eternal. They never asked that He be conceded a place at a table where a world conference on comparative religion was in session. They were not concerned about whatever modicum of truth "other faiths" might have to bring to the banquet feast of religion. Their Christ had *all truth,* was willing and anxious to feed as many guests as cared to accept His invitation, with loaves and fishes provided by Himself, hence it would be an affront to their host for a guest to offer supplementary courses.

There was but one seat of authority at their table, at the head where Jesus sat, and they all "sat at his feet," listening. They had no contribution of their own to make, they merely accepted what He gave out. That unquestioning faith in Jesus as One who had entered this world from heaven to reveal God to man will account for both their changed lives and their teachings. To them He was an atoning Christ, with authority to forgive sins, and they believed they would be anathematized if they preached any other gospel. Preachers today have no other authoritative message.

They were men of consecration. They "left all and followed him." Ministers now must do that also. Many ministerial failures can be traced to the preacher's holding on to something connected with this world—and Christ's "kingdom is not of this world." Some take the plow and look back. Some indulge a questionable habit. Some hang on to a distracting business connection. Some can not "leave all" because they are bound to a pleasure-loving or disinterested wife. Some seek "security" by dividing loyalties, scratching the ears of lustful supporters with compromising ethical philosophies or advocacy of conformity to worldly ideals and pleasures. Men thus handicapped should not preach.

They were men of proven character. The admonition to "take heed to" themselves was a demand they have a character void of offense to God and man. They were not scandal-mongers with a penchant for spitting venom in the direction of one not friendly to them. They were equable-tempered, "no strikers." They exercised self-control. Though they had consciences as keen as a hound's nose when pursuing sin, they were tender, sympathetic, loving, never breaking reeds bent with penitence nor treading out smoldering fires of love flickering in faltering hearts. They were generous, hospitable, free from covetousness.

We cannot think of them as running into debt and leaving for another pastorate with unpaid bills, bringing reproach upon the church and its ministry thereby. They "learned in whatsoever state they were, therein to be content." There is no record of their complaining of the stinginess of churches, of the inefficiency of official boards, of low salaries, or unfurnished parsonages. It is unlikely that they spent time regaling loafers with off-color anecdotes in lodges or on street corners.

They commanded respect by their Godly lives rather than to court it by sartorial con-

formity. They needed no tonsure, no low hat
with oval crown, no reversed collar, no alti-
tudinous vest, or pulpit robe, as a badge of
ministerial dignity. Their code forbade professional display or ostentatious parading.
They respected the wish of their Master who
warned against informing the religious left
hand what the right one was doing. Their
joy and reward were found in the fruitfulness
of their service.

They were cast in a heroic mold. To them,
martyrdom was a coveted road to immortality.
That spirit is essential still. Assuredly, this
is not time for a fawning "yes" man in the
pulpit. Sermon trimming should not be done
to provide more paper for salary checks. The
stench of disloyalty that rises to offend the
nostrils of Him who loves an odor of sweet
smell, can not be rendered pleasant by burning
incense to the surrealistic god "popularity."
This is a day when "tolerance" is exalted to
heaven, and "conviction" is denounced as "bigotry" by some who are first on their feet to
respond to a call for "men of light and leading."
It requires some courage to brave the ostracism
which is decreed in the seats of the mighty.
It is as true today as it was in Paul's time,
that "those who are reputed to be somewhat"
can not add aught to the message of a minister

who finds his message in God's revelation. But some make an attempt, too often successful, to compel the preacher to cower before a certain type of ecclesiastical tyranny which is as merciless as a gangster's code. Unless he submits to their yoke, he has no part or lot in "kingdom enterprises." His worth to the real kingdom of God, however, is gauged largely by his independence of human authority. The opinion may be expressed with some confidence that Christ will look with greatest approval upon the minister who refuses to wear any man's yoke, that he may be yoked up with his Lord alone; who refuses to be branded with any marks save "the marks of the Lord Jesus." Stephen is a good patron saint for preachers in this age.

New Testament preachers were not place-seekers; they were place-makers. Few of them could build on another man's foundation. They sought places where churches ought to be, rather than where they already were. They did not look upon the ministry as a "job." It was a "ministry." It is not probable that the Antioch church was flooded with applications for the pulpit from the twelve, or the seven deacons, when Barnabas and Saul left for Cyprus. It is pathetic, perhaps tragic, when a preacher manifests less desire to *build* a con-

gregation to the size which will give him sufficient support than he does in finding one
already able to care for him. Is it un-Christian
to affirm that one who is unable to build a
church is not entitled to support from one?
Why should any preacher, especially a young
one, expect others to bring him a desirable
pulpit as a sort of graduation gift, with a comfortable salary and "all the perquisites there-
unto belonging"? Does his education give him
a holy and inalienable right to support? Is
there any other vocation in which provision is
made for the continuing support of those who
fail to produce? There are acres of the vine-
yard of the Lord awaiting planting, pruning,
developing by capable vine-dressers.

Laborers are as badly needed as in any
age. Who will say, "Here am I Lord, send
me"?

The first preachers were driven by an urge.
"Woe is me if I preach not the gospel,"
described the feelings of others besides the
apostle to the Gentiles. "I am not ashamed
of the gospel," Paul wrote to Rome, and was
impatient to "see Rome," bringing it as his
message for the capital of the empire. "They
that were scattered abroad went everywhere
preaching the word." They simply could not
keep silent. It was a trial for them to settle

down long in one place. Other regions besides
Macedonia kept beckoning to them. They
preached even while enemies gathered stones
for their execution, calling on the Lord Jesus
to forgive the sin of their persecutors. They
were rewarded for that by seeing heaven opened
and the Son of man standing at the right hand
of God, awaiting the arrival of their spirits
upon the dissolution of their earthly taber-
nacles. If prison doors were opened, they went
out to continue preaching the same gospel
which authorities had forbidden them to proclaim, knowing that more severe punishment
would follow at once. Successful professional
men, like Dr. Luke, left their professions to
preach the unsearchable riches of Jesus Christ.
Talented youths like Timothy and Silas chose
the privations of the ministry instead of the
riches of this world. They were seeing the
things that are unseen and eternal. They
labored for the meat that perishes not. They
learned the secret of "possessing" through
"denial." All those early ministers had but
one passion—"Christ." One passion is quite
sufficient for the greatest soul on earth, provided that passion is for Christ.

Like their Lord, the New Testament ministers were "in the world but not of the world."
There is a sense in which the minister should

always be a "man apart." Not a recluse,
avoiding contacts with his fellow men, but
"keeping himself unspotted from the world."
He must associate with people, even wicked
people, but his mission to and with all men will
be the same: seeking to win them to his Christ.

In the home where sickness and death have
taken a toll from sorrowing hearts; where
despair has flooded out hope; where alienations
have forged chains of hate between brethren;
where doubt is mocking faith; in homes such
as these the minister will be found, not living
apart from others' needs.

But the very nature of his calling and work
necessitates his retirement from the world, both
in time and space, for certain recuperative and
in-filling experiences, where in prayer and Bible
study, meditation and reading, he may lay by
in store for future and further expenditure of
energy. In all his work, he must be a man
"apart" from all that we call "worldliness."

If he has a mission at all in ministering,
it is to guide and lead souls in this material
world in their preparation for an eternal world.

New Testament ministers had but preca-
rious support in their ministries. They were
worthy of their hire, and accepted it gratefully
when it was given. Paul thanked the Philippian
church for more than one offering which

brought him decided relief, permitting him to leave the tent-makers' bazaar and devote all his time to preaching. Others than he learned in whatsoever state they were therein to be content. If infirmity brought them to a dependent state, they trusted God and the brethren to feed a worn body until it became uninhabitable for the soul.

It is not on record that any of them resorted to the civil courts to collect salary debts. They preferred to suffer themselves rather than to have reproach brought upon the church.

No single characteristic of New Testament preachers is more notable than their modesty and humility. No boastful word appears in the records of their labors. Only occasionally, and then quite incidentally, are we informed as to the identity of those who built the great churches of that age. There were many such, for large and active congregations sprang up in widely scattered areas. But under whose ministry? Seldom is information on this obtainable. They all worked together in a common cause, giving no thought to pro-rating and distributing "credit" according to "kingdom achievement." The personalities responsible for success were not honored above other equally loyal and faithful, but less successful, coworkers. They did not advertise their own victories. Yet what opportunities they had for doing that! To illustrate: telegrams like the following coming in to the "Brotherhood News-Broadcaster":

"Jerusalem.—Pentecost Sunday. Great revival on. 3000 confessions first invitation. Continue."—Simon Peter.

"Ephesus.—Whole city shaken. Diana image makers put out of business. $2,500.00 worth of books on magic burned last night in public square. Corinth next."—Paul.

"Athens.—Spoke yesterday to executive group of Athens University. Two conversions. Great interest."—Paul.

"Corinth.—Masterly sermon last night by Dr. Apollos, graduate of University of Alexandria. Given unanimous call to pulpit just vacated by Paul."—Aquila.

"Joppa.—Baptized treasurer of Queen Candace of Ethiopia today. Azotus next. Wire for dates."—Philip.

It is legitimate, and an encouragement to others, to report progress in evangelism and church growth. But in disseminating such news, personal vanity should not obtrude, much less try to conceal itself behind such cellophane screens as: "To God be all the praise!" Jesus' "If any man would be great among you, let him be your minister," raises the question

whether some very famous preachers will not
be assigned to office-boy or feet-washing service
in His eternal kingdom; not because they are
bad men, but because they do not measure tall
by Jesus' standard of greatness. At times, it
would seem to be as hard for a talented minister to be humble as it is for a rich man to enter
the kingdom of heaven.

New Testament preachers were "called"
men. Some, like the apostles, by Jesus personally. They, however, constituted a temporary
group in the ministering order, and were chosen
for special duties. Others were called by them,
as in the instances of Timothy, Titus, Silas,
et al. Churches took the initiative in sending
men forth sometimes. It is but fair that those
who call a young man to the ministry should
feel a responsibility for his support. If he
yields to their persuasion, they owe him encouragement and help in his preparation.

In the event that a man takes it entirely
upon himself to decide as to his ability, character, fitness, etc., and enters the field without
urging or encouragement by others, there is no
responsibility on the churches to give him
support.

What constitutes a "call"? The gift of all
talent is a call from God to use it for Him, in
whatever capacity it can be made to serve His

cause best. Every man's native talent is stored
up in him while yet in his mother's womb.
When God desires a preacher or servant of the
church, he begins some thirty years before the
time for such ministry arrives by endowing an
unborn babe for the task. In the fullness of
time, he is brought forth and the training and
culturing of that talent begins. This is what
Paul had in mind when he wrote: "But when
it was the good pleasure of God who separated
me from my mother's womb, and called me
through his grace, to reveal his Son in me,
that I might preach him among the Gentiles"
(**Gal. 1: 15, 16**).

He does not affirm that God arbitrarily pre-
determined his career, but that God gave him
the qualifications (all that we know as personality) which, when trained and consecrated,
would enable him to accomplish the good pleasure of God as an apostle to the Gentiles. This
would seem to be Paul's conception of the first
step taken by God Himself in "calling" a man
to the ministry. Ability to minister is, therefore, God's first summons to service. "Ability"
as used here includes everything that goes into
the making up of the man—intellectuality, spirituality, devotion, willingness to endure hard-
ness, etc. One thus endowed may be certain of
his "call."

Following that comes a profound conviction that God will never be quite pleased with his life if he does not preach the gospel. It is the urge of conscience to do that which God would accept as a spiritual service.

The wise youth will counsel his best friends in Christ, not for approval, necessarily, but to obtain their candid judgment as to his fitness and opportunities.

He should enter upon the work believing sincerely that Jesus is the Christ, and that the Bible is inspired of God. That will give him a message of authority. Unless he has such a faith, common honesty, if nothing else, should restrain him from attempting to preach. Nothing is more pitiable, nor more contemptible and disgusting, than to see a man in the pulpit, pretending to be a minister of Jesus Christ, who has nothing but a human message to proclaim. It can never be more than a philosophical or speculative guess, and people need not maintain churches to hear an orator ask questions which no one can answer.

An accurate knowledge of what the message of Christ to the world is, is another indispensable pre-requisite to a call to ministering. Of course, technical and scholarly comprehension of it in all phases is not essential. That may be acquired subsequently. But an understanding of the fundamental teachings and program of Jesus, at least, must be present, for the Master would not ask one to go and preach that of which the messenger had no knowledge, or a perverted understanding of it. This paragraph may end with a recapitulated summary: that without talent, personality, character, knowledge of what the preacher should preach, unreserved loyalty to Christ, and a firm belief in the Word of God as God's inspired revelation, no one is ever called to preach. The young man who possesses these qualifications has received a call from Christ, by the very fact of their possession, and should heed that summons. He may venture forth into the ministry feeling that he, as well as those in an earlier day, is being sent of God. It may be thought by the reader of this paragraph that those who can meet the requirements are few. That is true. It is not denied that some men who have spent some years in ministering have missed their real calling. A misfit in the ministry is a source of grief to all concerned. But the number of such is not sufficiently great to create a problem.

The first ministers were trained men. They had a course in the best school earth has seen— that in which Christ Himself was the teacher. That He had the purpose of training in mind

is clear from the name He chose for them—
"disciples." They matriculated in His school
when they enrolled as "learners" or "students."

Their curriculum, so far as we know, was
not as extensive as that usually provided in
Christian schools now. But who knows how
much Jesus taught them, to correct false under-
standings of what we call science, philosophy,
economics, homiletics, exegesis, etc.? The fact
that they remained silent on these matters is
some indication that they had been put on
guard against making blunders which, in later
times, might discredit their teachings on religion. Their avoidance of everything pertaining to secular knowledge in their preaching is
too significant to have been due to oversight
or to accident. Notwithstanding the fact that
Jesus knew it all, He is not quoted as ever
saying anything which did not have direct
bearing on man's personal relations to God
and Himself, and man's moral obligations to
his fellows.

The same is true of all His inspired
teachers.

This fact should be a clear guide in curriculum preparation on the part of colleges and
seminaries designed to train men for ministering. Each generation has needs peculiar to
itself, hence the training courses for ministers

will vary somewhat. The major objectives in ministering can not be changed, for they were planned by the master Teacher for all time. But specific courses must be provided to assist the novice in service in the adaptation of his ministry to the demands of his own time.

A pertinent observation may be made here. Judged by the products turned out, some religious schools of the present devote less time to teaching the most important subject of all— the Bible—than to any other course. The absolute ignorance of the Bible itself on the part of some seminary graduates is appalling. They have spent years in hearing lectures on what some men (perhaps now dead) have speculated about it, but few weeks in acquiring a working knowledge of its content. The reason for this is, of course, that the teachers in these schools have lost all faith in the Bible as a divinely inspired Book of authority. With no authoritative text, they fill in time by training essayists, moral uplifters, book reviewers, or religious wanderers in the deserts of pseudo-scientific and ethical wastes. Nothing can be more tragic than to see a young man in the pulpit who has no message of authority. There may be some connection between the almost universal rejection of all the older sanctions in morals and defiance of all earthly governments, and the pulpiteering of the past few decades which derided the Bible as a revelation from God. Men who recognize no religious authority will not acknowledge authority in any other area of human interest.

It is highly desirable that the young man who enters the ministry today should have the most thorough education it is possible for him to acquire. Average intelligence and culture is at high tide for all time. The preacher must command respect by the accuracy and breadth of his knowledge. What he knows about history, science, psychology and other useful phases of learning will all be helpful for illustrative purposes, and if his hearers find him dependable in his allusions to such subjects, they will have greater respect for what he says about Christ and the Bible. But the real value of all secular branches of learning will be determined by the contribution it makes to the preacher's message about the Bible and its Christ.

The temptation to make this suggestion is too great to resist. No amount or degree of cultural training can be helpful in ministering if it raises questions instead of answering them, if it sows doubts instead of stabilizing faith, if it discredits the sources of Christian knowledge by degrading the inspired books to the level of

mere human documents, if it robs the student
of a divine Christ and leaves a moral reformer
in His place.

A distinguishing characteristic of the first
ministers, worth acceptance still as a model to
be closely followed, is the fact that they were
men with singleness of purpose and program.

To them, Christ was not *one* among others;
He was the only One.

His mission to earth was spiritual, intended
to restore man to right relationships with God,
through Himself as Mediator.

Those first preachers believed that. Knowing they had a monopoly on this work of reconciliation, they confined themselves strictly to
their specialty, never invading the realms
where economists, philosophers or politicians
legitimately wrought.

They were out to save men from sin. The
gospel was the only power capable of doing
that. It was God's power unto salvation in
the fullest sense and to the nth degree. They
tried no short-cut route to salvation, nor did
they hold out offers of material aid as a bribe
to discipleship. Everything in their ministering
was Christ-centered. The world would change
for the better rapidly now, if ministers would
devote their energies to that same objective,
wearing themselves to exhaustion in travel, and

travail, and teaching, and ministering, instead of devoting so much time to oiling ecclesiastical machinery and drawing plans for "world programs" which would be better left on the board with thumb tacks still in.

CHAPTER VII

The Minister and the Local Church

The minister, in whatever capacity he serves, such as preacher, teacher, pastor, executive, is what his title implies—"minister" (servant) to the congregation which supports him. If they minister to him in material things, he owes it to them to really minister in spiritual things. Before he "partakes of the things of the altar," he must minister, earning the right.

Heaven's industrial code provides for a fair basis of exchange—so much service for so much reward. The minister, as well as the tradesman, comes within the scope of that divine rule: "If any man will not work, neither shall he eat."

In all industrial situations, we have little difficulty in determining the status of a "servant." There should be even less in the church.

The minister's relation to a local congregation which has contracted for his time, is that of a servant, to whom certain clearly defined duties or obligations have been delegated.

His *"commission,"* of course, comes from Jesus Christ. It carries a command to preach the gospel as Jesus Himself taught it to His disciples. As an ambassador on behalf of Christ, he is obligated to proclaim the message as found in the divine Commission. If he fails to declare the full content of that Commission, he is a false ambassador, has repudiated his oath of loyalty to the King of heaven, and is guilty of breach of trust with the church.

He may serve some church with itching ears which desires a "just-as-good-as" gospel, anxious to conform to the world, by delivering denatured spiritual messages or leading in this-worldly activities, but he can not be a servant of Christ and do that. The one thing in his ministry from which a true preacher dare not vary in the least is the divine gospel as revealed in the Bible.

He does, however, have a commission from those who support him. In all his ministrations, he is a representative of the people constituting the group that ministers to him in material things.

When he delivers a sermon, he becomes the unitary mouthpiece through whom the group speaks. He is not to "speak from himself,"

unless he frankly states that he is doing so.
His hearers have a right to assume that he
represents accurately the views, teachings,
ideals and programs of the congregation with
which he is connected. Unless he does that,
he is more of a criminal than the man who
obtains goods from a business house under
false pretenses. Dishonesty in religion is worse
than dishonesty in trading. There is a fine
point of honor involved here which not all
ministers "honor." Some have sought a pulpit
from which to proclaim doctrines or specula-
tions which they have reason to know the congregation would not approve, withholding or
even misrepresenting their own beliefs during
negotiations. The Jesuit conscience is not confined to Roman clerics.

The intellectually honest man will state his
theological views without hesitancy or equivo-
cation. If they are at variance with those
which the congregation holds, he should, in all
honesty, seek another location. In a very vital
sense, he is the church's representative, and if
his public utterances do not express the religious beliefs and attitudes of those with whom
he is working, he should be indicted by the
grand jury of public opinion, convicted of ministerial malfeasance, and denied further pulpit
endorsement.

He calls in behalf of the church. His visits in the home are more than an expression of his own personal interest. They should be that, certainly, but wherever he goes on pastoral missions it should be made clear to those he serves that he is the personal embodiment of the good will, sympathy, concern, love, felt by the congregation he represents.

The needy, the unfortunate, the discouraged, the heavy-hearted, the sick, even the erring, will hold him in no less esteem if he tactfully assures them that the church is ministering to them through him. They will have an increased affection for the church and its divine Head when they find the spirit of Christ in him as he ministers.

When some phases of shepherding or oversight are delegated to him, he acts in behalf of the church in what he does.

As its minister, the congregation has a right to assign work to him in those areas of Christian duties where his talents or training qualify him to render more efficient service than others in the church are able to perform. He should do whatever he can do better than others and encourage others to do what they can do as well or better than he.

There is one kind of ministerial activity which must be carried on continually—that of evangelizing. The infusion of new blood renews its youth. If such transfusion brings the blood of a "new creature" into the veins of the church, its continued life is assured. That is a "type" of blood which harmonizes perfectly with that of all true Christians. Evangelizing by "teaching and persuading from house to house"; by personal interview; by letter or tract; and always from the pulpit, has Scriptural authority.

This is the special field where the minister must become all things to all men that he may win some. Personal problems, instances in which obstacles must be removed, corrective instruction concerning the beginning of the Christian life, these and similar situations can be met and handled best by personal interviews.

Converts that are personally won by hand-picked methods seldom fall away. Even that part of ministering in which "perfecting of the saints" is prominent in sermonic objective, the message may always be presented with both evangelistic fervor and appeal.

No worship service should be closed without the invitation having been extended. Many happy surprises await the minister who habitually ends the sermon with the invitation, regardless of the particular purpose of the address, with a fervent exhortation to confess

Jesus as Christ. Earlier preachers were masters of persuasion and appeal from the pulpit, and the success they experienced should encourage more thought and emphasis on that division of an ideal homiletic creation than is usually given to it today.

The preacher, in the sermon of that special worship period, may not provoke serious thinking on the necessity of being a Christian, but some one may be there who has already reached a decision, and is merely waiting for the invitation to be extended.

There are many well-written tracts about Christ and the church available, all of which may be helpful in reaching people in their homes. More ministers should prepare a tract setting forth the particular program of the local churches to which they minister. There is a more definite appeal in a tract which outlines the faith and purpose of a local congregation than in a general abstract one. People who may not be interested in what a particular group of churches stand for, are interested in that particular congregation which is established in their neighborhood.

The preacher who is not evangelistic will be preaching to vanishing audiences, unless he frequently supplements his own work with that of specialists in the field of evangelism. There

is a returning appreciation of the need for
evangelists who know how to persuade men to
begin the Christian life. The day of the special-
ist in evangelism is not over. Should that day
ever come, it will be when every local minister
has mastered the art—a rather remote possi-
bility. The church was born at the end of an
evangelistic sermon in which the preacher "with
many other words testified and exhorted, saying, Save yourselves from this crooked generation." Success in evangelism brings a holy
glow into the heart of a devoted minister, adds
to his ministerial stature, multiplies his influence and protects him from gloom and despair.

Ministers who are successful in evangelism
are never pessimistic.

There was a pardonable joy in the hearts of
the seventy when they truthfully reported,
"Even the demons are subject to us in thy
name." Why should they not rejoice? If a
minister, or a church, emphasizes one thing
above another, by all means let that be evangelism, either at home or in other communities.

In his pastoral work the minister is, more
directly, the personal representative of the
eldership. The New Testament churches were
cared for by their bishops, or elders. It is
fitting, wise, conducive to good order and Scriptural, that the minister should be under the

supervision and work in harmony with the eldership of the church he is called to serve. To be sure, he serves the entire group, but their chosen representatives in carrying out the will of Christ are the elders, a sort of committee entrusted with the spiritual oversight of the congregation. What they are unable to do, either because of inability or lack of time, the minister does by their authority. The relation between the preacher and the eldership should be one of the most cordial and sweetest fellowship. If it be, unity in the congregation is assured. Without it, but limited success may be expected.

Among the duties the minister has to meet in his pastoral work is that of "calling" on the membership. Often these demands either make or break the preacher. On whom, when, how often, shall he call? Some very successful men outline a time schedule for that phase of their work to which they adhere quite rigidly. Weeks or months in advance, they can refer to the date book and tell where they will be on any certain day.

Calling, as they view it, is routine work. If that be the best plan and especially if it succeed, no word of criticism should be offered. But is there not a danger that work so done becomes a mere routine in itself and misses the real

objective in pastoral visitation? It is, of course,
desirable that the minister be in as many homes
as possible, for his entrance should be a benediction.

But is it necessary, or even desirable, that
he call at homes where no special reason for
such attention exists? Should he not be relieved
from unnecessary calling to give his time to
pressing demands arising out of real needs?

On whom, then, should he call? First, on
the sick, the infirm, the shut-ins, the aged, the
troubled, the discouraged, the bereft. What
an opportunity he has to minister to all such!
Into their lives he may introduce a new hope
and comfort. They greet him with tears; he
leaves them assured that loads have been
lightened. He can help them to see that even
sorrows may be transmuted into joys; that
despair may be but the evening before the
morning when new courage rises; that the
weak in body may be mighty in spirit; that
bereavement often transplants hope from earth
to heaven. The visitation of a Godly man in
homes where needs like these exist is like that
of the angel who ministered unto Jesus. It
drains the vitality of the visitor. He will often
feel like Jesus did, when the woman in the
crowd "touched him," exhausted, knowing
that "virtue had gone out of him." But he is

reassured in the knowledge that the energy he has lost has merely passed into the lives of others who needed their spiritual vitality restored.   It is conserved.

Sympathetic and tactful pastoral ministrations endear the preacher to those whom he serves, perhaps more than anything else.   As he exalts Christ in the homes where he is a guest, his own personality and calling are magnified also.   This phase of service no true minister can afford to neglect.

A question as to prior duty arises at times. What service can the minister render in the home where the family is under quarantine? His first obligation is to "minister" to them, as to any others.   But unless some special need demands it, he should not be expected to violate a quarantine law by entering the home, for he may become a carrier of the disease to another home in which he calls.   He can, however, write a letter of sympathy and encouragement, assuring the family that the church is remembering them in their isolation.   He can also call at the home and make inquiry at the door.   He should certainly do more than use the telephone.

The advent of a baby in a home always opens doors through which the minister may find entrance into hearts.   A call in the hospital or at the home, as soon as discreet wisdom suggests, is imperative. If the family has been careless, he can congratulate them on the providential placing of an innocent life in their hands to be nurtured in the fear and admonition of the Lord. If the family has no church home, he may establish a bond between them and the church by obtaining permission to enroll the baby in the Cradle Roll Department of the Bible School. Seldom will this request be refused. Later, the baby may bring the family to church.

The practice of leading in a "ceremony of dedication" at the birth of a baby is of very doubtful propriety. It has little religious merit and no Scriptural sanction. At best, it is but a cheap substitute for infant baptism. Rarely do parents who understand the New Testament teaching about the church wish any such service. Requests for the ceremony usually come from those who look upon it as having Christian approval and esteem it of spiritual value in the life of the child. An hour spent in informing the parents concerning the place of baptism and its relation to church membership will disabuse their minds of un-Scriptural notions, and lead them to see that there can be no efficacy in any religious act in which the central figure in it can have no personal part, except by proxy.

The minister is the logical one to make approaches to new families moving into the community served by the congregation.

An early call upon strangers, with an invitation to attend services and a brief tactful word about the objectives and program of the local congregation he serves will introduce the minister to the newcomer favorably and open the way for further indoctrination, if needed or acceptable.

The minister should keep careful check on the attendance at various services. He needs to know not only the number who are present, but *who* they are. If members of the congregation are absent, an early inquiry as to the detaining cause will serve a double advantage. He may be helpful in a situation of which he has not been informed; and people feel complimented when they are "missed." They must be of some importance, else their absence would not be noted. If the absence has been without good reason, that is the first notice served by the vagrant that he is about to backslide. The surest way to recapture a backslider is to prevent his slipping! The minister can find no better company for his leisure moments, if any, than in the presence of novices in the Christian life, especially if the babe in Christ has much to overcome. When first indications of looking back appear, the glory of that which is ahead and its incomparable advantages over what is behind, may be pointed out and moral lapse prevented.

Every congregation has its "problem folk." Some have an inferiority complex, usually revealed in their having been "slighted."

The preacher dare not tell such (except in rare cases) that the only trouble, in reality, is that they themselves have been carrying a heavy load of pride, and some good friend has tried to relieve them of its weight. Those easily "peeved" and "overlooked" always have inordinate pride, though always professing great humility.

Some are habitual "exaggerators." They do not mean to falsify, but nature gave them eyes that magnify. The preacher soon learns the percentage by which their statements must be discounted.

The gossip is hard to silence. Malicious tales and surmises are a poisonous flow from a fountain of envy and jealousy; or are emanations from impure minds which, because of certain inhibitions, must enjoy sin vicariously. Sometimes the gossip is a case for discipline.

Some try to monopolize the time of the minister that they may be made to appear as his favorites. Others never like to see him lonesome, so drop in during his study hours to "help pass away a little time"—good souls.

At times there is a tremendous temptation to deliver a pulpit broadside against all and sundry such. But patient forbearance will produce better results. Even people with most annoying weaknesses have souls to save, and the church must always conduct a clinic for them. Many of these are "babes in Christ," not in years, but in spiritual growth. A Christian with "religious rickets" is more pitiable than a child physically undernourished. Perhaps the spiritual malnutrition from which these victims suffer is due to the diet prepared and served in the pulpit. In that case the preacher should take care to add the proper vitamins.

Ministering to the bereaved is one of the most important phases of the preacher's work. When asked to conduct the religious part of a funeral service, he should visit the home of the deceased at once and assist in every way possible. Perhaps in making arrangements. Perhaps in comforting. Perhaps in turning a spirit of rebellion to one of submission. Whatever help may be rendered by attention at such times, will never be forgotten. The conduct of the service does not fall within the purpose of this lecture.

Within a few days after the funeral, a call should be made in the home to assure of continued sympathy and to help in making the readjustments which a death always necessitates. No other situation offers so many opportunities for helpful ministry. In sharing the sorrows of others, the minister is as nearly Christlike as he can hope to be in this life. Jesus shared sorrows, none of which were His own, and was "made perfect by the sufferings He bore." It was probably the sufferings of others, rather than His own, the bearing of which perfected Him. It is a heaven-sent privilege to suffer as Jesus did. The minister also will find it a perfecting experience.

What is the duty of the minister to the local church so far as its financial program is concerned? Shall he keep hands off entirely? Shall he lead in it, or manage it? Much depends on local conditions. In this area, as in all others, he is a "servant."

His support comes from the church, and he therefore has a legitimate interest in the "laborer's hire." But his ministry must be carefully guarded from every appearance of commercialism or covetousness. He does have a commission from the New Testament to teach its doctrines on stewardship. That may be done at such times and in such manner as to neutralize any criticism on the theory that he has too strong a personal interest in the offerings.

The delicacy and tactfulness he displays in meeting his stewardship responsibilities is usually a criterion by which his whole ministerial ideals and leadership may be judged. The less he has to do with details of collections of money the better. Likewise with its distribution. Except in rare instances, he should refuse to handle any of it except his own salary. If he be compelled to be a custodian for any of it, he should insist on strict secretarial accounting for every penny. No minister should ruin his life as a preacher by carelessness in receiving or expending church funds.

More important still are the personal financial habits of the minister. Many good men have discounted their influence, sometimes to the point of liquidation, by contracting debts, failure to meet obligations on time, unwise spending, etc. Nothing, except a charge of immorality, will more surely cripple the work of the preacher than to gain a reputation for financial carelessness or crookedness. Never should he contract a debt unless he knows whence his payments are to come. The fact that the church may owe him sufficient money to pay his bills does not excuse him for failing to meet them on time. Such a situation may be a seedbed for bringing reproach on both himself and the church.

If unable to meet a legitimate obligation, the minister can always find some one who knows him who will make him the necessary loan.

If no one has that much confidence in him, he should not be in the ministry. Usually, if he be honest and frugal, some member of the congregation will gladly give him a monetary accommodation.

A very practical, and sometimes disturbing, problem for the local minister to decide is what amount of time, if any, he shall give to outside agencies seeking his services, on the ground that they are "community enterprises," or agencies for uplift, reform movements, etc.

It is not always easy to decide. The first obligation of every man who is supported by an organization is to that group. The preacher's primary duty, then, is to the church he serves. His response to the numerous calls that will come to him must be determined by what the net result of his acceptance will be in the interests of the church. Some very worthy causes depend largely upon ministerial promotion. Unless he is sure that his activity in and support of an enterprise will help in building up the church of Christ, he should beware of yielding to the importunities of those who seek his cooperation because it costs them nothing.

More than once, well-intentioned preachers have been drawn into movements ostensibly of a reform character, to learn later that they have been deceived and tricked. One alliterative organization of that nature will occur to the mind at once. It is most unfortunate when a preacher finds himself in the embrace of some "reform" Delilah, who shears him of his influence of good name even before he has time to slumber in her lap. Nothing can be lost by deferring participation in a new movement until its leadership as well as its aims have been thoroughly investigated.

The above paragraph leads to a further consideration and emphasis on the fact that a minister's first duty, both to Christ and the church, is to *build up the local church*. Some who are unsuccessful in doing that, for one reason or another, become active in every local organization or undertaking, thereby concealing from some their failure as preachers, and take pride in being "kingdom builders." Only in the rarest instances (in fact no authentic case has yet been cited) is a "kingdom builder" a successful "church builder." In other years, preachers were concerned chiefly with evan-

gelizing and culturing the local church. They
were inspired with a holy enthusiasm by the
fact that Christ never spoke with more confidence nor with more prophetic voice than when
He declared He would build it, and protect it
from all assaults, even to the gates of Hades.
In His program it was to be "the pillar and
ground of the truth," of which He was the
personification. Formerly, preachers were persuaded that Christ loved the church and gave
Himself for it; they also loved it. Christ died
that it might be; they lived that it might continue and flourish. He purposed that it should
be a "glorious church, without spot or wrinkle
or any such thing"; they labored to keep it
above reproach. Christ, as Lord, added to it
daily those that were being saved; they brought
the new recruits of salvation to Him. The
manifold wisdom of God was to be manifested
in the church. Christ was its Head, and they
tried to keep His body functioning in His
behalf, after His ascension, as His own body
had done during His earthly life.

That Christ still loved His church after
His glorification was demonstrated, as they
saw it, by His coming back to walk among the
candlesticks — local congregations — revealing
His abiding concern for it and His yearning for
continued fellowship with its worthies, unwor-

thy though they might be. Persuaded of its divine origin, made courageous by the pledged victory for it, challenged by the heroic demands it made upon them, preachers of yesterday literally gave their lives to the building of Christ's body, collecting the individual units of it and cementing them together in local groups for co-operative work in introducing His kingdom. They devoted all their energies to obeying His command: "Go, teach, baptize, teach." Multitudes were added under that regime. The same faith, loyalty, zeal, which characterized those earlier ministers would add new multitudes today. It would seem that this should be the supreme task of the church and its ministry.

As one of the shepherds or "pastors" of the local flock, the minister bears a heavy responsibility for keeping the congregation "united in the bond of peace." It may be well to remind ourselves that the New Testament treats Christian unity as a local problem.

No New Testament writer visualized a great dominating ecclesiasticism as Christ's ideal for a united church. That conception is of political and papal origin. One of the most amazing anachronisms in present-day Christian thought is the perpetuation of papal ideals in various forms, though it anathematizes their source.

The idea of an organized union is an outstanding example. The unity Jesus prayed for was a spiritual one between Himself and His followers individually (**John 17:21**). The units in His ideal unity are individuals, not sects, organizations, groups, etc. It was His desire, as understood and emphasized by Paul in his Epistles, that there should be no groups, parties, factions, denominations, etc. Therefore, the only way by which the prayer of Christ can be answered will be by the disintegration or disappearance of all groups, parties, denominations, because every one of them is a divisive device of Satan. Many may disagree with this statement, but before rejecting it hastily, kindly go through the New Testament again and check the teaching: that no minister has a responsibility for Christian unity wider than the area, or congregation, in which he is serving. If he keeps that group Scripturally united, he has met his full obligation.

His jurisdiction does not extend beyond that border. If, by his teaching and ministrations, he prevents factionalism arising in the church he serves, and keeps it loyal to Christ in both doctrine and life, all working together in carrying out His program, he is a good minister. If division exists elsewhere, he is not responsible.

A word should be said relative to the beginning and ending of a ministerial service with a local congregation.

What factors enter into a beginning? First, of course, is the call from the congregation seeking his service. That should be nearly enough unanimous that he can begin with assurance of helpful, sympathetic, Christian co-operation on the part of the church. Occasionally a disaffected minority may be won, but it is perilous to count upon that.

A frank understanding as to compensation, always regulated by living costs and conditions, is due both parties.

That being satisfactory, the minister then needs to ask himself prayerfully whether he is able to meet the demands and opportunities of the field. If he hesitates, it may be a point in his favor, for it indicates that he has a sense of moral responsibility to meet the needs and expectations.

No greater mistake can be made than for a minister to accept a call when ability, training, personality or health are inadequate to the task. Failure disheartens the preacher and disappoints a hopeful congregation—a tragedy in either case. No devoted minister should permit his ambition to lead him to assume a responsibilty too great for his ability.

What about the time tenure? It should usually be indefinite, permitting a termination at any time, with fair notice, if either party to the contract should consider a change advisable.

But so long as the relation continues to the mutual satisfaction of all concerned, neither should seek a change. Most great churches have been the result of long continuing ministries. Churches demanding frequent change become hard to please, critical, cynical, selfish, unfair.

Preachers who hold short ministries never build an enduring work. They are likely to become "sermon repeaters," cease growing, become exacting in their demands upon a congregation, and permit a spirit of pessimism and restlessness to ruin a ministry.

When a proper time arrives for the termination of a ministry, the preacher has the opportunity to leave the field well prepared for a successor, or to leave it in such a condition that even an apostle could not lead in a successful work. Nothing provides a better criterion by which to judge the real spirituality and Christlikeness of a preacher than his conduct and spirit as he yields a ministry, especially if some pressure has been brought to bear upon him to do so.

He can, if really big enough, so ingratiate himself with all whom he is leaving, that they will regret his going—and may invite a return after awhile!

So long as a ministry is fruitful it should continue. When it becomes unfruitful, it should terminate.

CHAPTER VIII

The Objective In All Ministering

There is unity of purpose in the divine objective and program of ministering. Varying orders of service are provided for different responsibilities assigned to different officers, but they are all integral parts of a harmonious whole, as conceived by Christ, for the achievement of His aims in coming to earth.

Apostles, prophets, evangelists, pastors and teachers, each with some special duty to perform, but all working together under the authority of Christ, have been charged with the task of making known Christ's will to men and leading in the work of realizing it among men.

In **Eph. 4: 11-16** Paul has stated this objective in a mighty crescendo of logical sequences. It begins with an enumeration of the orders Christ has authorized for ministering, and ends with a "body building itself up in love." In all ministerial labor and in adopting every method used for its success, that ultimate goal of ministering must be kept constantly in mind.

The first stage of ministerial endeavor on the part of the officers named is "the perfecting of the saints." "Perfecting" is a sanitary word. It means "to render fit, sound, complete; to mend; to equip, put in order, arrange, adjust," etc. The underlying idea in it is that of restoring one to what he should be in his religious life. The one to be "perfected" is already a "saint," "one set apart" to the service of God, hence he has been evangelized and accepted discipleship. The ministry of "perfecting" consists in supplying proper spiritual food for growth in grace and knowledge of the truth, and in directing daily exercises in Christian virtues, and in giving corrective treatments for all religious and moral abnormalities. It takes the lost son who has been found and instructs him how to behave in his new position in his Father's house.

Old associations with sin must be broken off and new acquaintance with righteousness made. It is not easy to "perfect" even a "saint," but when accomplished, there is great reward for it.

Even so meritorious an accomplishment as the perfecting of an individual is not an end in itself. That achieved, immediately another

assignment confronts him. His "perfection"
for service must be demonstrated by "ministering." Again, that divine plan of first doing,
then teaching, comes to the fore. Ministering
appears to be about the only work He has
entrusted to man about which God feels a con-
tinuous and anxious concern. Serving is man's
normal life. Spiritual health can be preserved
only by living devotedly in the areas of service.
Even Jesus came "to minister," and that He
might be successful therein, He "took upon
himself the form of a servant, being found in
fashion as a man." When He donned humanity, it was done that He might be attired becomingly in servant's livery. When He commanded
wind and wave, when He withered an unfruitful tree with a word, when He scourged the
oxen and scattered the coins of grafting temple
robbers, He displayed a consciousness of
princely authority derived from His heavenly
inheritance. But in all these He was not so
regal, as measured by His own standard of
greatness, as He was when He tied a plain
towel about Him and went the full round of
twelve ambitious dining guests, washing their
unworthy feet. When He accepted the cross,
He probably gave a more impressive demonstration of God's love for man. But He gave
the highest expression of man's love for his

fellows when He, as man, stooped to render a service so menial that none of the twelve would humiliate himself to perform it.

Ten thousand oratorios in praise of service have been sung by chanting worshipers, but all their varied harmonies sustain and emphasize the haunting beauty of that obligato melody of service in a Jerusalem upper room. How long is it going to take to induce the world to give more than mouthing assent to the truth that earth's greatest soul is the one who serves God and man most unselfishly? World peace, with every blessing which would follow in its train, is awaiting the day when men act in harmony with this truth; and we reveal our pitiable credulity if we expect it to arrive one day sooner.

Not even ministering, however, is an objective in itself. That is for the purpose of "building up the body of Christ"—His church. A problem in structural engineering in spiritual things is introduced to us here. "Building up" is the word which describes the process of erecting the house complete, above the foundation.

The foundation, Jesus Christ, is already laid. The blue prints for building His church are simple, easy to read, and no essential detail is omitted therefrom. It is needless to remark that they are found in the New Testament. Christ knew what He desired His church to do and to be in the world. Everything connected with it He outlined in plan, and His Spirit has written a history of the first work done on the building by men who were Spirit-filled and Spirit-guided. Both instruction and illustration are recorded there, that we might have all the necessary information for our own building labor. All ministering, including that of Christ, His apostles, the prophets, the evangelists, the pastors and teachers, in the first century was for the purpose of building up Christ's church. So should all our ministering in this century be directed. Christ's church has rights. It has duties to perform which only a strong, vigorous body can accomplish. But we have come perilously near devoting our time and energy to making the church serve a vague something we call "society," or "the industrial order," or mere "humanity." Ministering which is approved of Christ is in behalf of His *church,* and the primary obligation of a minister is to it, instead of to "society" or to any other humanly conceived program. The church should not be a caudal appendage to anything. It is a body, and entitled to the best of everything within the power of its ministers to bestow. Here is a fact which should sober sincere ministers: The church will be built up into just such a structure as its ministers make it. If they follow the divine plans, it will be just the kind of church Jesus desires. If they deviate from His instructions in any degree, to just that degree will it be displeasing to Him. He will not be comfortable or satisfied with His home unless it is built as He purposed. The addition of a "lean-to" shed spoils its beauty. Erecting walls to separate His "living room" into many compartments, instead of leaving it as one large "assembly room" for all His saints, mars the fellowship He desired His family to enjoy. These cheap sectarian partitions which men have insisted on erecting are not "sound proof," and unneighborly opinions of neighbors on the other side are frequently overheard, thus affecting domestic peace in disastrous fashion. The church should be a temple, not an apartment house.

This observation leads us to consider the objective of the church, for not even it is an end in itself. Paul declares that in it "the unity of the faith" is to be expressed, and manifested. Unity is an electric word these days. There is a temptation to parody a famous quotation and exclaim: "O unity, what crimes have been committed in Thy name!", however. A hundred conceptions as to what it is essen-

tially, and as many schemes for its attainment,
are being broadcast from pulpit, by radio, and
in the press.

One conceives it as a great dominating
organization, and enlists as a recruiting officer
for his own ecclesiastical group in the hope
that it may be permitted to do the dominating.

Another looks upon it as being realized in
a federation of more or less independent groups,
retaining their autonomy in small matters, but
surrendering it to some representative control
by the federation in "the larger interests"—as
if it could be agreed upon as to what they are.

Others think of it as a comity arrangement
in which all worshipers may come together
under one roof, leaving all their convictions
in an anteroom as they enter, and submitting
meekly to whatever may be provided for them
in the way of a social or worship program,
worked out by a steering committee repre-
senting all faiths and no faith. The unity
possible under that arrangement is a oneness
in surrendering. All must surrender something, none gain anything. Those who seek
that sort of unity can not be richer spiritually
thereby, for the content of their faith has not
been increased or purified. On the contrary,
all entering it become impoverished to some
degree, for they either yield some belief or hold

it in abeyance. Those with no convictions whatever might be measurably satisfied with the plan,
but such folk can scarcely be called religious. It is
a perilous experiment in faith to surrender a
conviction until compelled to do so by the
teaching of the Word of God, for it lowers
one's resistance to error and renders him indifferent to truth.   Tolerance of that which is
wrong is a doubtful virtue.   It is a travesty
on the unity Jesus prayed for in His church
when a group of worshipers agree only in
disagreement.   It is not the "unity of faith,"
but a unity in unbelief.   No great achievement
in any realm of human interest has ever
resulted from agreeing to disagree.   Try to
picture the state of a government operating
under such a political regime.   Imagine the
success of a bank which conducted its business
by insisting that its directors, in forming its
policies, avoid everything which any one of
them held to be vital to safe banking procedure,
and unite merely in petty details.   Enterprises
that succeed are always directed by officials
working under a maximum of agreements on
fundamental principles and procedures.

Since the New Testament has made so very
emphatic that which Christ insists upon as a
basis for unity, there is small excuse for ignor-
ing or flouting His wish.   The passage under

consideration declares that the purpose of all
ministering is to realize "the unity of the
faith." It is something very definite, for two
definite articles are used in the phrase. "Unity"
itself is a word of definite content, as used in
the Scriptures. It means "unanimity" or "agreement." The unity, therefore, must be on agreements. And to be effective, it must be unanimous. Therefore, ministering is for the purpose of bringing Christians into unanimous
agreement on and acceptance of "the faith."
What can that be but the "faith" which was
everywhere preached, believed, obeyed, by those
early Christians? One careful reading of the
New Testament writings will disclose it. All
the inspired men, whose preaching is recorded,
delivered the same doctrine, viz., that "Jesus
is the Christ, the Son of the living God."
Whether they addressed Jews or Gentiles,
ignorant or learned men, good men or bad men,
their message was always and everywhere iden-
tically the same. When those who heard it
were convinced and accepted it, they were
united in "the faith."

It is not dogmatism to affirm that no real
unity can exist where there is disunity on this
cardinal creed. Two can not walk together
except they agree, and in the church, men must
walk together to please Christ.

On the other hand, where there is unity on this creed, it is inexcusable to have division. Unconditional acceptance of the deity of Jesus Christ compels the believer to search the Scriptures to know His will, and guarantees instant and loving obedience thereto.

Where that simple faith, or creed, is the only basis of fellowship an ideal state of unity should exist. Christ's claims as to His personality, His authority to forgive sins, His program for worship and daily living, His promise to return, raise the dead, and reward His faithful followers all are accepted as corollaries to His demonstrated deity, and those who believe that may be assured of a united fellowship in doing His will.

"The faith" is intelligent. It is based on "the knowledge of the Son of God." Again, this brings to our attention the importance of a teaching ministry. It also suggests that Christ Himself constitutes the Christian curriculum. Christ-centered teaching, if intelligently and fairly presented, will inevitably produce faith in Him, in the hearts of all honest hearers.

But not even yet is the end of all ministering reached. All that we have noticed in this program thus far, has been projected that the Christian may become "a fullgrown man, unto the measure of the stature of the fulness

of Christ." Christ remains central in all ministering. Here, His majestic greatness as "a
fullgrown man" is before us as a model. Man-
hood, at its best, may be seen in Christ. An
obligation therefore lies upon the church and
its ministers to exalt the Christ before those
who would become truly great. If they fail
Him in this matter, the whole world will lose
Him. It is the "knowledge of Christ" alone
that will rescue the "children tossed to and fro
by every wind of doctrine." An expressive
figure this. How easy to persuade and move
children who, by nature, are credulous. The
child in years may outgrow his instability, but
the mature "child" who is ever seeking "some
new thing," or the one who becomes enraptured
by mystical pronouncements which he can not
understand, and concludes that they must therefore be profound, is the one to give us deeper
concern. How many are being led away from
Christ by one or more of the multitudinous
cults which employ every modern means for
indoctrinating the gullible with their absurdi-
ties! Magazines, books, tracts, radio broad-
casts, public lectures, personal interviews, etc.,
are used with alarming success by "zealots
without knowledge." How shall the situation
be met? The only practical way is to emphasize the fullness and all-sufficiency of the faith

that is in Christ. If one has "The Truth," he need not be ashamed to confess ignorance of error.

The ultimate goal of all ministering is that of building up the body of Christ in love. Every Christian is an individual member of that body, with organic functions to perform. Love, stripped of that sentimentalism which is no real part of it, is active obedience to Christ as a divine Lord. "If any man love me, he will keep my commandments" is Christ's measuring rod for estimating love. He who keeps His commandments loves Him. He who does not keep them, does not love Him. There is no middle ground for a neutral in this matter.

The conclusion of the matter is that the objective of all ministering is to bring men and women into covenant relations with Christ, by an acceptance of His gospel, then to train them in the knowledge of His will, that they may render Him obedience in every act of life. It is a simple program. But it is the greatest trust committed to men. This is a ministry to be exalted.